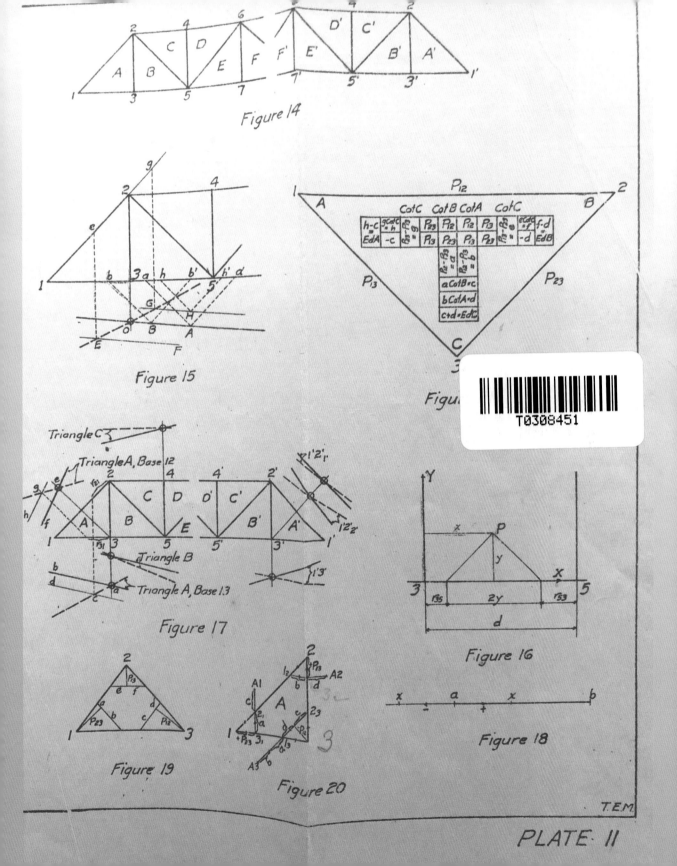

Figure 14

Figure 15

Figure 17

Figure 16

Figure 19

Figure 20

Figure 18

PLATE II

T.E.M.

For further information, contact:
Tumblehome, Inc.
201 Newbury St, Suite 201
Boston, MA 02116
https://tumblehomebooks.org

Library of Congress Control Number 2019940380
ISBN-13 978-1-943431-49-6
ISBN-10 1-943431-49-3

Noyce, Pendred
Engineering Bridges Connecting the World /
Pendred Noyce - 1st ed

Book design Yu-Yi Ling
Published in Boston, Massachusetts, U.S.A.

10 9 8 7 6 5 4 3 2 1

ENGINEERING BRIDGES

Connecting the World

Makers and Engineers Series

Pendred E. Noyce

CONTENTS

Shaharah Footbridge, Yemen

1

Bridges and Civil Engineers

IN THIS BOOK I'D LIKE TO TELL YOU about the fascinating world of bridges.

About how people built them long ago and how they build them today.

About some truly amazing bridges, like the Glass Bridge and the Winking Eye Bridge and some of the highest and longest bridges in the world. I'll show you different kinds of bridges, from simple beams and arches to complex suspension and cable-stayed bridges. We'll talk about the techniques people employ to build bridges and the materials they use.

You'll read about some surprising, terrible bridge catastrophes, like the Tay Bridge Disaster and the Quebec Bridge collapse.

You'll also meet some amazing people, such as the Tibetan "Madman of the Empty Valley," the self-made Missouri engineer James Buchanan Eads, and the steadfast Emily Warren Roebling, who helped her husband build the Brooklyn Bridge.

Why do I love bridges? First of all, because of what they do. Bridges cross gaps. Millions of them connect us together, all over the world.

Second, bridges bring out the best in human problem-solving. Each one addresses a particular challenge. How can we span this space? What kind of bridge will fit the landscape? What materials should we use? How can we make it last?

Third, bridges let us see how progress comes from a constant interplay of materials and methods. For thousands of years, people have been figuring out how to build longer, stronger, higher, safer and more beautiful bridges. New ways of building and new materials make new designs possible. Think of giant floating cranes, tempered steel, reinforced concrete, or computer modeling. I'll be telling you about all of those. All of them allow people to build bridges that once would have been impossible.

Bridge design is the job of civil engineers. Engineers figure out ways to build things and solve problems. Civil engineers design structures for modern water systems, transportation, and waste disposal. They create bridges and roads, railways and dams. Civil engineers figure out how to supply clean water and how to treat sewage. They analyze structures for safety and think about how to protect the environment.

This book is inspired by a pioneering Chinese civil engineer named Mao Yisheng (MOW ee-SHUNG) 茅以升. In 1912, when Mao was a sixteen-year-old student, China rebelled against the last Qing emperor to become a free republic. Four years later, with a fresh degree in civil engineering, the twenty-year-old Mao traveled from China to America. After a year at Cornell University, he came to Carnegie Mellon University in Pittsburgh, Pennsylvania, which is known as the City of Bridges.

Mao fell in love with bridges. At age twenty-three, he graduated from Carnegie Mellon as that university's first PhD student. Mao's doctoral dissertation—the research report he wrote to help earn his degree—analyzed stresses on frame construction. Basically, he studied how to make sure structures don't fall apart as you build them.

In 1919, with his head full of ideas, the young engineer went home and used his new knowledge to help his country move forward. He designed modern bridges and buildings, taught engineering to university students, and wrote books on engineering and the history of science. Throughout decades of political change, he kept his eye on one goal—building the structures of a new China.

There's even a statue of Mao Yisheng on the Carnegie Mellon Campus. Here it is.

Statue of Mao Yisheng at Carnegie Mellon University

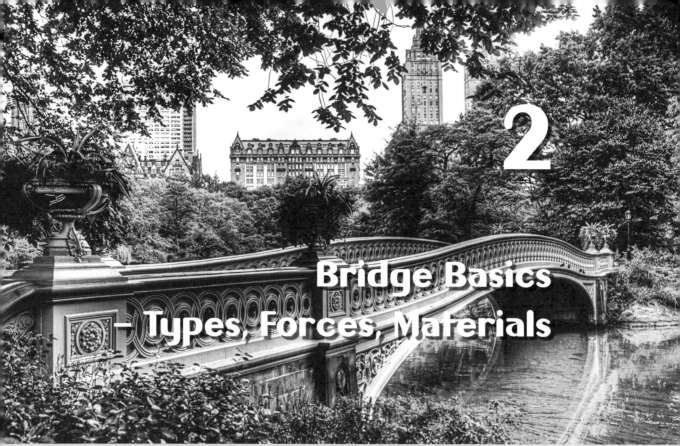

2

Bridge Basics – Types, Forces, Materials

Bow Bridge, Central Park

Who built the first bridge? And what are bridges all about, anyway?

Somewhere, thousands of years ago, a band of our human ancestors came to a stream and looked for a way to cross it without getting swept away. They maneuvered a log into place, made sure the ends of it were stable, and helped their friends and family set one wobbly foot in front of the other above the water. At the time, they didn't realize they had become the world's first civil engineers.

Over time, people grew more ambitious. They wanted to cross wider, wilder rivers, even deep gorges. Some wanted roads they could drive wheeled vehicles over. For building materials, they used whatever natural materials they could find—wood, stone, even grass.

A **bridge** is a structure that spans a gap, usually over a river, a harbor, a canyon, or a highway. The challenge is to build something strong enough to allow people, animals, vehicles, or sometimes just water to cross safely.

First, the bridge has to hold up its own weight without collapsing. That weight, with nothing on the bridge, is called the **dead load**. Believe it or not, some bridges fall down before anyone even tries to cross them.

Add the weight of people, animals, and vehicles crossing the bridge, and that's called the **live load.**

Bridges start from a few basic designs. Here are the most important.

Beam bridges, like that very first log bridge, have long, straight planks, logs, or beams that cross a gap, supported at each end. When the beams are especially long ones made of concrete or steel, they are often called **girders.**

Cantilever bridges are structures built with one end anchored or supported, while the other end sticks out into the open air. Think of a diving board. Many styles of bridges can be built with cantilevers from each bank of a river or gorge reaching out to meet in the middle.

Arch bridges have walls that curve inward from vertical sides to meet in the middle.

Truss bridges are made up of various bracing bars arranged in stable triangles.

Suspension bridges hang from ropes or cables tied between towers.

Pontoon bridges allow people to cross bodies of water along a series of floats.

In **cable-stayed bridges**, diagonal cables slant down from one or more towers to support the bridge.

You can also find variations and combinations, like

Tied-arch bridges

combination arches and cables, and more

Some bridges move. A part of them lifts, swings, or slides out of the way, usually to allow a ship to cross beneath. Drawbridges, bascule bridges, lift bridges, rotating bridges, or sliding bridges all act this way. We'll look at some of these bridges in Chapter 5.

Forces

Bridges have to withstand several different kinds of forces, including compression, tension, torsion, and shear.

Compression occurs whenever the bridge material is being pressed together or squished under the load of the bridge. Consider the weight of a truck compressing the columns holding up a bridge. Or consider a simple plank bridge built of one or more boards. When you stand in the middle of the bridge, your weight presses down on the wood directly under your feet, compressing the wood fibers in the plank.

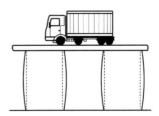

Tension, which is a force pulling the bridge material apart, is the opposite of compression. When you stand on the plank bridge, your weight bends it in the middle. It sags. Underneath the bend, the wood fibers are being lengthened and pulled apart. If the wood fibers get pulled all the way apart, you may find yourself dumped in the river.

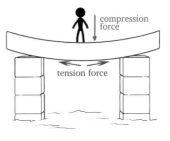

Bridges, especially suspension bridges, can also twist in the wind. This twisting force is called **torsion**.

Strong tides, raging rivers, or other forces can slide one part of the bridge, for example the lower end of the posts holding it up, in a different direction from another part. This sliding force is called **shear**.

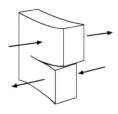

Weight, water, wind, and weather all exert wear and tear on bridges. Eventually, after years or centuries, any bridge may fail and collapse. Part of the job of a civil engineer is to ensure that the bridges we rely on stay safe. We have to be able to predict when bridges are beginning to be unsafe, so we can repair or even replace them.

Materials

People have used all sorts of materials to build bridges, including:

wood	tree roots	copper
stone	iron	tin
brick	steel	concrete
rope	rubber	plastics

What has allowed people to build longer and stronger bridges over time? Three things: new materials, new designs, and new construction techniques. In this book, I'll show you examples of all the designs and materials listed above. At the same time, I'll explain advances in building techniques, and we'll get to know some of the engineers who made these advances. Along the way, we'll discover both engineering triumphs and catastrophic failures.

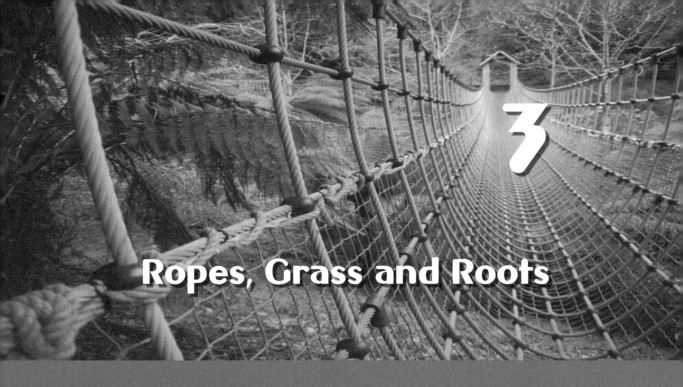

Ropes, Grass and Roots

Bridge builders throughout history have turned to the material closest at hand.

I MENTIONED ABOVE THAT THE FIRST bridges were beam bridges, probably logs laid across a gap. But the three bridge types I talk about in this chapter are probably also very ancient, even though they don't show up in written records until recent centuries. All three types can be made with materials the builders find close at hand.

Rope bridges

Before the Spanish conquerors set sail from Europe, the Inca Empire (1300s to 1572) stretched from the Andes to a strip of land along the western coast of South America. It was the largest, richest empire in the Americas. Yet the Inca lacked wheeled vehicles,

and they had no horses or donkeys to ride. Human runners had to trade goods and messages along roads that crossed gorges and climbed mountains. Lightweight, sure-footed llamas and alpacas served as pack animals.

The Inca road system consisted of two major north-south roads with numerous branches. In all, it stretched nearly 40,000 kilometers (25,000 miles), rising from sea level to over 4,500 meters (15,000 feet) in altitude. Most roads were 1-4 meters (3-13 feet) wide. The roads were laid with massive paving stones, and many of them remain today. In the sandy desert lowlands, the Inca built short walls to keep sand from drifting onto the roads. In the steep mountains, they built giant staircases.

But the Inca also needed bridges. Log bridges could span narrow gaps, and to cross marshy areas, runners simply threw down stones or floating reeds. For some rivers they used boats. But in other places, high in the mountains, deep ravines interrupted the road. With no wood nearby for bridge building, the Inca turned to rope.

To make the rope, the people wove together straw and grasses, which were light and easy to transport. They suspended long ropes of these woven grasses between **anchorages** on either side of each ravine. In cross-section, the bridges looked like Vs, with two handhold railings and a narrow footpath made of woven matting at the bottom. Side ropes reinforced connections and helped keep people and animals from slipping sideways off the bridge.

However, with frequent use, a rope bridge quickly begins to sag. Wind, sun, and rain also take their toll. After one or two years, villagers had to burn and replace the bridge. Repairing bridges was part of the labor tax Inca subjects owed to their rulers. As you can imagine, bridge building over deep ravines was a dangerous job, and many unlucky laborers fell to their deaths.

Q'iswa Chaka, Peru

Today, only one such rope bridge remains. It's called the Q'iswa Chaka, which in the Quechua language means "rope bridge." Every June, it is rebuilt by local residents keeping old traditions alive, in a ceremony to honor their ancestors and the Earth Mother.

Bamboo Bridge, Cambodia

On the opposite side of the planet, in Cambodia, stands another bridge that local people build and replace every year. This one is built of bamboo. The bridge between Kampong Cham and Koh Paen island is about 300 meters (1000 feet) long. It crosses the Mekong River during the dry season, when the river is low—too low for ferry boats, but still too high for people to cross on foot. Then, just before the rainy season starts in May, the people take the bridge apart before the rising river can sweep it away. During the rainy season, villagers cross the river by boat. Meanwhile, they store the bamboo to use again the following year.

Bamboo is a fast-growing member of the grass family. Some species can grow almost a meter (3 feet) a day. Although light and rickety-looking, bamboo is actually incredibly strong. Along its length it has a compressive strength greater than wood, brick, or

Kampong Cham (here and facing page)

concrete. Its tensile strength—its resistance to being pulled apart—is close to that of steel.

Building the Kampong Cham bridge each year requires about 50,000 pieces of bamboo. First, villagers drive long bamboo stakes into the river mud. Using thin lengths of flexible bamboo as ties, they lay bamboo beams across the top of these stakes. Then they roll bamboo mats out along the entire surface.

When finished, the bridge is strong enough to carry people, animals, motorcycles and even trucks. People crossing the bridge pay a toll—a few cents for locals, and forty times as much for foreign tourists. In this way, the bridge pays for itself.

Living Root Bridges

The warm and humid northern Indian state of Meghalaya may be the wettest place on earth, with more than 11 meters of rainfall a year. Rivers rise and roar through small gorges between villages. The gaps are not long enough to require bridges of steel or stone, and wooden bridges would quickly rot in the humidity.

Villagers have come up with a unique solution. Along the river banks grow hundreds of specimens of the rubber fig tree, Ficus elastica, which shoot aerial roots out sideways from their trunks. Villagers guide these roots across the river, sometimes just through the air, sometimes on a scaffolding of wood or bamboo. The skilled bridge makers weave the roots together or even graft them with roots crossing the gap from the other end. Over time, as the tree grows, the roots thicken, so with the passing years, the bridge grows stronger.

What's amazing about the bridges is that making them requires such patience and teamwork. It may take years of nudging and weaving to build a bridge. But if the trees that anchor it are healthy, the bridge can last for hundreds of years.

How the tradition of living root bridges started is unknown, but the first western report was written by an English lieutenant in 1844. There are even double-decker bridges or parallel bridges with two walkways side by side.

I've never crossed a Meghalaya bridge, but I bet the rain-soaked roots are slippery!

Living root bridge, Meghalaya

4

Early Stone Arch Bridges

ROPE BRIDGES DON'T LAST LONG, AND LIVING root bridges can only be built in a few places on earth. The major advance in ancient bridge-building was the invention of the strong, durable, stone arch bridge. The oldest bridges still standing today are stone arch bridges. Here's one of them.

Arkadiko Bridge

Ancient Greeks of the Bronze Age, also known as Mycenaeans, built the Arkadiko Bridge out of huge pieces of limestone fitted together without any **mortar** or **cement**. Later Greeks said the stones were so huge only monsters like the one-eyed Cyclopes could have lifted them, so the philosopher Aristotle called these stones Cyclopean stone.

The Arkadiko Bridge was part of a highway between two cities. The roadway was probably built of packed gravel and dirt. At 2.5 meters (about 8 feet) wide, the bridge allowed a single chariot to rattle across the gap. You can see how difficult it would be for a chariot to cross the gulch without a bridge, even though the bridge is not very high.

Take a close look at how the Arkadiko Bridge was built. It used the **corbel arch** design.

Arkadiko Bridge

As the builders stack the stones on each side, they make each higher row stick out a little farther into the gap, until at the very top, the two sides almost touch. Then it's easy to cover the final gap with just one more stone. This is not a true, self-supporting arch. Protruding towards each other, the walls tend to fall inward, so the sides need to be very thick and strong.

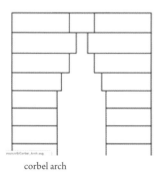

corbel arch

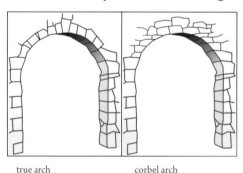

true arch   corbel arch

Imagine standing facing a friend with your arms up. As you lean towards each other, and your raised palms meet in the space between you, you form a human arch that will stay up as long as each of you keeps the other from falling forward into the space between you.

Alcántara Bridge

The next major advance in bridge-building was the development of a self-supporting arch, also known as a voussoir arch. (We'll call it a true arch.) The top part of a true arch is a semicircle built of slightly wedge-shaped stones that carry the load out to each side and down onto thick stone columns.

Let's look at a bridge built on true arches, the Alcántara Bridge across the Tagus River in Spain. The Roman emperor Trajan ordered his engineers to build this bridge between 104 and 106 C.E. Twelve local towns contributed to the cost. The builders even constructed a triumphal arch across the roadway to celebrate Trajan's victories in war.

Six arches span the Tagus. Take a close look at any of them. At the very top of the arch is the keystone. Instead of lying atop a gap between two leaning sides, the keystone fits right between the last, highest wedges from each side. It looks as if it might fall straight down into the river, but it is held in place by the two sides of the arch, which, leaning together, squeeze it between them. In turn, the keystone presses against the two sides, keeping them from collapsing into the middle. In fact, that precarious-looking keystone, which is very slightly wedge-shaped, is what holds the whole arch together.

Alcántara Bridge

This is the keystone. In many arches, it will be larger and more tapered.

Besides the true arch, two other innovations were crucial for building a bridge like the Alcántara. The first was the discovery of a waterproof **cement** that could stand up not just to rain but to river water. The Romans found that if they mixed together water, lime, sand, and the powder of volcanic rocks or tuff, they could create a cement they could easily smear on rock surfaces. Once the cement dried, it took on a rock-like hardness and strength.

The second invention was a method for building below the water surface. The Romans constructed waterproof wooden enclosures called **cofferdams**, double rings of wooden stakes driven into the riverbed. Workers packed clay into the space between the two rings, making a waterproof wall. Then they pumped or bailed out the area in the middle. Within the space that dried inside, construction workers could build a foundation for a bridge **pier**—one of the columns or towers that held up the bridge.

Usually we think cement has to dry out to turn hard. But the Roman cement could set, or harden, even under water. A chemical reaction between the dry ingredients and water made the cement stick together and harden. The technical term for cement that can harden underwater is hydraulic cement.

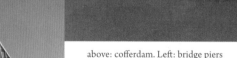

above: cofferdam. Left: bridge piers

Segovia Aqueduct

Aqueduct of Segovia 1824 Edward Hawke Locker

The Romans were the first to recognize the full power of the stone arch. The Segovia **Aqueduct**, built in Spain, exemplifies another important innovation, the two-tier or two-story design. One arch stands directly above another, so the weight on each upper column is transferred straight down to a lower column.

Built around 100 C.E., the Segovia Aqueduct extends for 15 kilometers and runs as high as 28.5 meters above the ground (94 feet, more than nine stories high). The aqueduct is built of granite blocks. Because they are cut so precisely, these blocks stay together without any mortar or cement.

It's like one cheerleader standing on another cheerleader's shoulders.

"Aqueduct" comes from two Latin words meaning "water" (*aqua*) and "to lead" (*ducere*). The stone archways supported channels that carried water from mountain streams to homes and cities. Roman engineers carefully designed each aqueduct to descend just a few feet per mile. The slow, smooth, continuous descent meant the water flowed steadily, without the need for pumping. Aqueducts supplied fountains, baths, and sewage systems, bringing the luxury of running water to people many, many miles from the source. The longest Roman aqueduct ever built was the "Eiffel Leitung" from high in the Eiffel mountains of Germany to the city of Cologne (95 km or 59 miles).

At intervals, engineers built **cisterns** or tanks into the waterway. These tanks allowed silt and debris to settle out of the water so the channels stayed clean. Dirt sank to the bottom of the tank, while clean water overflowed into the next section of the aqueduct.

Most of the length of Roman water systems ran in pipes underground, just like water systems today. But sometimes topography, which is the rise and fall of the land, made elevated waterways more practical. By the third century C.E., almost 29 miles of aqueducts supplying Rome ran high above the ground on arched channels like the Segovia Aqueduct.

Eleven aqueducts supplied Rome with about 300 million gallons of fresh, clean water each day. That was probably more than 300 gallons for each resident of the city.

Pont du Gard

Sometimes a bridge carried both a road and an aqueduct, like this one, the Pont du Gard in Nîmes, France. In the first century C.E., the Romans built this three-tiered aqueduct to carry water across the Gardon River in ancient Gaul.

To build the Pont du Gard, Roman engineers wrote out their plans on wax tablets. Then they cut limestone into shaped blocks. Using cranes and block-and-tackle pulleys, they moved 50,000 tons of limestone pieces into place.

After the fall of the Roman Empire, the aqueduct channel became

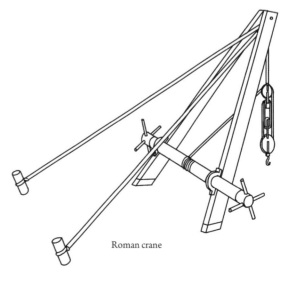

Roman crane

clogged with brush and dirt. Water stopped flowing. However, the bridge survived as a toll bridge, with people paying to cross it.

The fact that this beautiful stone bridge has lasted nearly two thousand years shows us the immense strength of arch construction. It also shows that stone is an ideal material for building arch bridges. Stone is easily available, and it has very strong compressive strength. Unlike wood, it can bear great weight without being crushed or squashed.

The Pont du Gard aqueduct descends by only one inch from one end to the other—just enough to keep the water gently flowing. Amazing! Can you imagine how precise the Romans' measuring tools and building techniques had to be?

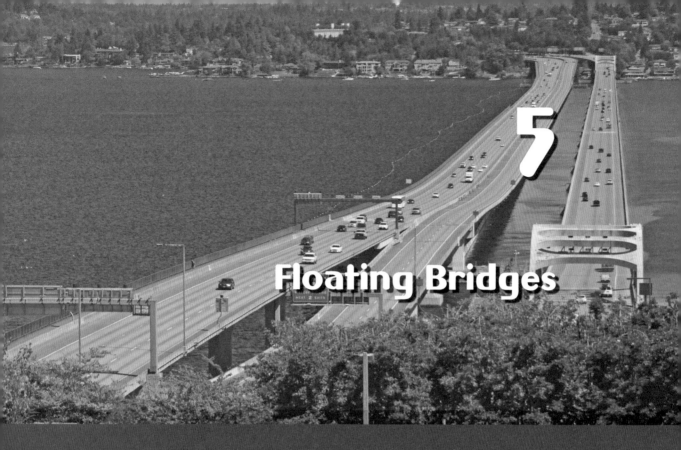

5

Floating Bridges

Usually, we think of a bridge rising high above the road or body of water it's crossing. But a bridge can also float directly on the water.

Suppose you're a general who needs to get your army across a river or narrow sea in a hurry. Ferrying your troops one boatload at a time will take too long, especially with all the trouble of loading and unloading horses, vehicles, or heavy equipment. What you'd really like is a kind of walkway along the top of the water.

In 480 B.C.E. Xerxes the Great, Emperor of Persia, faced this problem when he reached the Hellespont. The Hellespont, or Dardanelles Strait, is the waterway at the head of the Aegean Sea that separates Asia from Europe. Xerxes was on his way to invade Greece, but first his army had to cross this mile of open water.

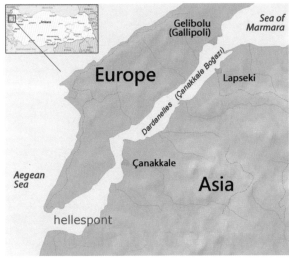

Map of Hellespont

According to the Greek historian Herodotus, Xerxes ordered his engineers to construct a pair of temporary crossings, two floating or **pontoon** bridges, across the Hellespont. Xerxes' men anchored 674 low-slung warships side by side in two rows all across the strait, using unusually heavy iron anchors at the bow and stern of each ship. Then the engineers strung cables

A pontoon is a supporting float filled with air.

made of papyrus and flax across all the ships from shore to shore. Men at both ends used **windlasses**—turning winches—to tighten the mile-long cables.

Then, says Herodotus, soldiers laid wooden planks across the tightened cables and added brush and earth for a roadway on top. When the swinging, lurching roadways were ready, men, horses, and baggage spent a solid week streaming across the bridge. Herodotus says there were a million men; modern historians estimate Xerxes had about 60 thousand.

But how much can we rely on the tale from Herodotus? Did the Persian army really cross a mile-long pontoon bridge? While Xerxes' army certainly

Xerxes crossing the Hellespont by Edmund Ollier

did cross the Hellespont, modern engineers have questioned details of the story. They have pointed out several problems. In the deep strait, the anchor lines would have been too long to work well. Ships would have swung, collided, and tangled in the current. Manufacturing one long rope a mile long to cross the water would have been well beyond the technology of the time, and windlasses alone could not have been strong enough to tighten such a long and heavy cable.

More likely, the Persians anchored a long row of boats, rather than the more expensive warships, in smaller groups, two or three at a time. Then these small links were tied together to form a long, wavering line. Wooden planks probably connected each boat to the next, rather than resting on two long cables above the decks.

Whatever the actual configuration of the bridges, the army managed to walk above the water from Asia to Europe. Xerxes defeated the Spartans at Thermopylae and burned Athens. However, a few months later, the Greeks destroyed his navy at Salamis, and Xerxes scuttled home in defeat.

Xerxes was not the only ancient commander to lead his army across water. Chinese generals were probably using pontoon bridges to cross rivers by the 8th or 9th century B.C.E., if not earlier. Military engineers tied or chained

Dongjin floating bridge in the 1940s

a row of boats together and then laid planks over the surface of the boats. People and horses walked along the swaying road while water lapped below. Most of these bridges would have been temporary, but one bridge from the Song dynasty (960-1279 C.E.), Dongjin Bridge, survives today. No doubt the boats and planking are replaced often!

Armies have turned to pontoon bridges again and again. Around the year 170, the Roman emperor Marcus Aurelius crossed the Danube in central Europe on a bridge of anchored boats, as shown in the picture below.

In the late 16th century, the Indian emperor Akbar even led his elephants across a pontoon bridge. Imagine what it must have been like for the elephant drivers, trying to keep their animals steady and calm on the rocking roadway!

Roman pontoon bridge, Column of Marcus Aurelius, Rome

Akbar's Adventures with the Elephant Hawa'i in 1561

Throughout history, engineers experimented with different materials for building pontoons. A pontoon had to be large, relatively light, and waterproof. In the 1600s, the French developed copper pontoons. During the American Civil War, Union army engineers covered wooden frames with tin or copper, canvas or India rubber. Canvas pontoons were especially useful because they could be prefabricated and were light enough to carry in army wagons.

During World War II, the Allied invasion of Europe required numerous river crossings as soldiers attacked through France,

Belgium, and Germany. Invading tanks and armored vehicles carried prefabricated parts that allowed American military engineers to construct bridges rapidly. Sometimes engineers used inflatable floats made of rubberized canvas. For heavier loads, they used pontoons made of aluminum **alloy.** Across these floats, engineers laid treadways, steel tracks that could carry heavy trucks or even tanks. Engineering battalions could build about 50 feet of treadway per hour.

Because they block river traffic and are buffeted by tides and currents, most pontoon bridges are temporary. Still, there are some permanent pontoon bridges in use today, and we'll read more about them in Chapters 14 and 17.

*A person building a pontoon bridge has to think about **Archimedes' principle**: The buoyant force of a pontoon is equal to the weight of water it displaces. Buoyant force is an upward force. It has to be able to counteract the weight of the pontoon itself, the overlying roadway, and any people and equipment crossing.If the bridge needs to support more weight, engineers have to make the pontoons larger and lighter.*

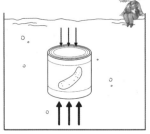

US Army crossing the Rhine on heavy pontoon bridge at Worms, March, 1945

6

More Stone Arches
(Anji, Ponte Vecchio, Rialto, Si-o-se-pol)

Anji (Zhaozhou) Bridge

But enough about pontoons. I want to tell you about just a few more famous and beautiful stone arch bridges.

Anji Bridge (Zhaozhou Bridge)

THE OLDEST BRIDGE STILL STANDING in China was designed by a craftsman named Li Chun during the Sui dynasty, about 1400 years ago. The beautiful Anji or Zhouzhou Bridge crosses the Xiaohe River in Hebei province in southeastern China.

The Sui emperors dedicated themselves to great public works projects to unify their empire. They constructed two capital cities and excavated the Grand Canal, a 2400-kilometer waterway connecting the Yellow River and the

Yangtze. The Anji Bridge (Anji means "safe passage") was a much smaller project, but it was important to improve the ease of trade in the southern provinces.

In a major innovation, the Anji Bridge did not use a full semi-circular arch as the Romans did. For the first time, Li Chun used only 87 degrees instead of 180 degrees of a full arch. This meant the ends of the arch pressed back against the river banks at an angle. For this reason, the bridge required strong **abutments**, built-up structures at each end of the bridge that keep the ends from sliding outwards. The bridge itself is built of limestone pieces connected by iron **dovetails**.

Another innovation of the Anji Bridge is its open **spandrels**. The spandrel is the triangular space between the outer, upper edge of an arch and whatever it is supporting above, in this case the bridge walkway. Leaving this space open decreased the overall dead weight of the bridge and gave it a light and airy appearance. Just as important, if the river flooded, high water could flow freely through the open spandrels, decreasing shear pressure on the bridge itself. The open spandrels may be one reason this bridge has lasted for over 1400 years.

A Tang dynasty official who viewed the bridge seven decades after it was built recorded his admiration.

> Its convexity is so smooth, and the wedge-shaped stones fit together so perfectly... How lofty is the flying-arch! How large is the opening, yet without piers! [...]Precise indeed are the cross-bondings and joints between the stones, masonry blocks delicately interlocking like mill wheels, or like the walls of wells; a hundred forms (made) one.

Because of its graceful shape, Ming Dynasty poets described the Zhaozhou bridge as "a long rainbow hanging on a mountain waterfall" and "a new moon rising above the clouds."

dovetails

Ponte Vecchio

The Ponte Vecchio, or Old Bridge, crosses the River Arno in Florence, Italy. Originally, it was a Roman bridge of stone and wood. Twice, floodwaters swept the bridge away. In 1345, the bridge was rebuilt in the form that still stands today.

The Ponte Vecchio has three segmental arches with closed spandrels. Shops have always crowded both sides of the bridge's walkway. During the Renaissance, butchers, money changers, and merchants sold their wares on open tables. If a merchant fell behind on paying his debts, soldiers might storm in to break up his table and end his business. The Italian phrase for broken table, *banco rotto*, is thought to be the origin of our word "bankrupt."

In 1565, the Grand Duke Cosimo de' Medici wanted a way to walk easily from the town hall to his personal palace on the other side of the Arno. The streets were full

Cosimo I de' Medici, Grand Duke of Tuscany

of unruly mobs that didn't appreciate the nobleman who had taken away their liberties, so Cosimo had his builders create a private, enclosed walkway called the Vasari Corridor. The corridor ran along and through various buildings until it crossed the river, protected within the upper story of the Ponte Vecchio.

Once the corridor was ready for use, the duke banned butchers from the bridge so he and his guests wouldn't have to smell the stink of aging meat. As the butchers departed, goldsmiths moved in. Today, the Ponte Vecchio is still lined with shops selling fine jewelry and metalwork.

During World War II, the retreating German army, which had occupied Florence, destroyed all the city's bridges except the Ponte Vecchio. The German field marshal spared it not only for its history but because he judged it too old and weak to support his enemy's tanks and artillery. He figured that the Allies wouldn't dare to use it to come after him. However, just to be sure, he blew up buildings on both side of the river to block access to the Ponte Vecchio.

Here's one case where being considered old and weak was an advantage — for a bridge!

Rialto

Another Italian stone arch bridge with a history of ups and downs is the Rialto of Venice. Venice is a city of islands set in a lagoon. Over a hundred canals thread the city, criss-crossed by 391 bridges. City traffic is an interplay of speedboats, water taxis, and gondolas below and tourists and Venetian pedestrians above.

In 1180, an engineer named Niccolò Barati built a pontoon bridge across Venice's widest canal. The presence of the bridge helped the Rialto market grow to the point that a larger bridge was needed. This second bridge was built of wood, with two ramps climbing to a central section. When a tall ship approached, the central section could be raised so the ship could pass. As on the Ponte Vecchio, shops sprang up along the sides of the bridge.

However, the wooden bridge suffered its share of disasters. In 1310, a disgruntled nobleman named Bajamonte Tiepolo led a conspiracy to overthrow the Doge of Venice. When stopped and defeated in the Piazza San Marco by forces loyal to the Doge, Tiepolo's gang retreated. They burned the Rialto Bridge behind them.

The bridge was rebuilt, but in 1444, it collapsed under a crowd of people watching a boat race. A similar accident occurred in 1524. The Venetians began talking about replacing their rickety wooden bridge with one built of stone. In 1531, city leaders officially invited architects to submit their designs.

Antonio da Ponte's name means "Anthony of the Bridge."

Several famous architects, including Michelangelo, competed for the chance to build the new bridge. Most of the plans involved several arches anchored in the river, but they would clearly interfere with navigation. Finally, Antonio da Ponte claimed that a single partial arch could span the canal. Other architects doubted the safety of his plan, but da Ponte won the competition.

The bridge took three years to build. Work was completed in 1591. Set on 12,000 wooden **pilings** sunk into the mud below the canal, it consists of a single partial arch tall enough to allow galleys, the long Venetian rowing ships, to pass beneath. Two stepped ramps lead up to a **portico** supported by columns and arches of its own.

The bridge proved to be sturdy. In 1797, soldiers fired a cannon from its steps to break up a mob, with no structural damage. Today, the bridge is a tourist highlight of Venice, so much so that it has even been a target for a terrorist attack. In 2017, three men from Kosovo were arrested for plotting to bomb the bridge.

Si-o-se-pol, Isfahan, Persia (Iran)

What happens to a bridge when the river it crosses dries up?

The Safavid shahs of Persia ruled from 1501-1772. Great patrons of the arts and architecture, they also established Shi'a Islam as the state religion of Persia.

1598, Shah Abbas I founded the city of Isfahan as his capital on the Zayanderud, which means "life-giving river." This river, the largest in central Persia (which is now Iran), flowed from the Zagros mountains to end in a swamp or seasonal salt

Detail of Masjed-e-Shah Mosque in Isfahan, ordered built by Abbas I.

lake southeast of the capital. Fish thrived, and Persian engineers tapped water from the river to irrigate crops and supply houses upstream. The capital grew.

As fine houses multiplied on either bank of the river, the shah decided he wanted a beautiful bridge to cross it. He turned to his top official, Allah Verdi Khan, who had been born a Christian in Georgia near the Black Sea. Taken prisoner by the Persians as a young man, Khan converted to Islam and joined the shah's army. He rose through the ranks of Abbas I's service to become a governor and eventually commander-in-chief of the army. The shah entrusted him with everything from assassinating troublesome ministers to suppressing rebellions to building bridges.

Khan assigned an architect named Mir Jamal al-Din Muhammad Jabiri

to design a bridge to please the shah. The bridge has 33 pointed stone arches on its first level and at least double that many on a second level. Built of limestone and brick, the bridge is just under 300 meters (almost 1,000 ft) long and 14 meters wide. Niches along the side gave pedestrians a place to sit,

Si-o-se-pol, Isfahan, Iran

sip tea, and view the river. And the bridge served another practical purpose, as a seasonal dam. Sluice gates could be opened or closed to let high river water flow through or to hold it back.

But by this century, the Zayanderud was in trouble. Too much water was being siphoned off upstream, mostly for agriculture but also for heavy industry and private homes. Add in a drought, and by 2014, no river ran under the bridge. Today, in place of waves reflecting lamps at night, there is only a wasteland of chalky dust.

Periodically, the Iranian authorities talk about restoring the river. Perhaps a tunnel could bring water from another part of the mountains to meet the needs of businesses and homeowners. If that happened, a massive green building project might transform the space. But for now, the dry, cracked riverbed remains.

The bridge's name, "Si-o-se" means "thirty-three."

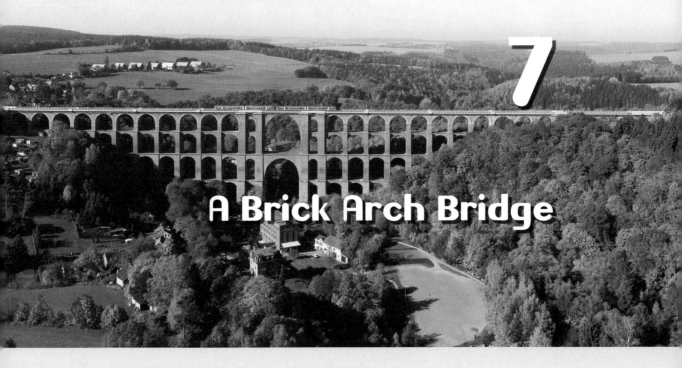

7

A Brick Arch Bridge

Göltzsch Viaduct 1851

TODAY, ARCH BRIDGES ARE OFTEN MADE OF STEEL OR concrete. People have seldom constructed bridges of brick. But sometimes it is most convenient to use a material that can be found or made on the spot.

In 1845, the Saxon-Bavarian Railway Company announced a competition to design a bridge across the Göltzsch Valley between Saxony and Bavaria, which at the time were two separate German kingdoms. The prize was 1000 Thalers (about $24,000 US today), and 81 people submitted entries. However, none of them could prove that their designs would stand up to the load and stresses of railway trains crossing the bridge. So the chairman of the prize jury, Professor Johann Andreas Schubert, decided he would design a bridge himself. He used the new science of **structural**

analysis, which allowed him to mathematically analyze the pulls and pushes on every part of the bridge.

In order to keep costs down, Schubert decided to build his enormous bridge of brick. It was an unusual choice: everybody knew bridges were built of limestone and granite. But stone is expensive to quarry and transport, while good brick-making clay lay all around. Schubert decided granite would be used for only a few key points along the bridge.

People have been making bricks for 9500 years. The earliest bricks were made of sun-dried earth or clay. Later, people added straw and fired their bricks in kilns. By the time Schubert designed his bridge in the mid 1800s, bricks could be mass produced. In fact, twenty brickworks set up in the Göltzsch Valley and produced 50,000 bricks, each exactly the same size, every day.

If the brickworks worked for 400 days, how many bricks does the bridge have in all?

Wooden scaffolding for the arches required at least 23,000 tree trunks. Altogether, the bridge employed 1636 workmen, thirty-one of whom died on the job, mostly through falls or falling bricks. When the Göltzsch Viaduct was finished in 1851, it was the world's tallest railway bridge at 256 feet. Today it is still the longest, largest brick bridge in the world.

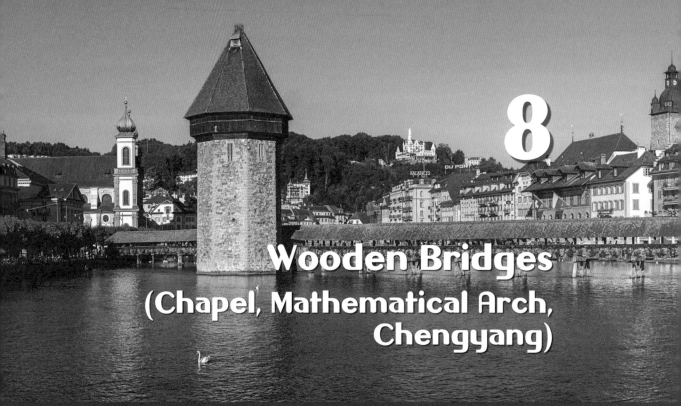

8

Wooden Bridges
(Chapel, Mathematical Arch, Chengyang)

STONE IS GREAT FOR BUILDING BRIDGES, BUT IT'S HEAVY and hard to work with. For centuries, wood has been easy to find, easy to cut and shape, and easy to move. But wooden bridges don't last as long as stone bridges. They rot too easily, especially when they're wet.

One way of protecting wooden bridges from rain, snow, and hail is to put roofs over them. Early colonists in America built covered bridges throughout New England, though few of them survive. Here is another, much fancier covered bridge, one of my favorites: the Kapellbrücke or Chapel Bridge of Luzern, Switzerland.

The Kapellbrücke (Chapel Bridge)

The Kapellbrücke is built diagonally across the River Reuss in the city

of Lucerne (Luzern) in central Switzerland. The bridge was first built in 1365 as part of the city's defenses.

In 1332, Lucerne helped form a Swiss confederacy to support free trade and peaceable relations along trade routes through the Alps. By 1353, the confederacy had eight member towns prepared to defend them-selves in battle against the powerful ruling Hapsburgs. Lu-cerne's town fathers decided to build a wooden footbridge to connect new and old parts of the town. That way, defending sol-diers could run to the part of the town that most needed them. The bridge faced the lake, from which an attack was most likely to come.

*A **trestle** is a frame with a horizontal beam joined to two pairs of sloping legs. Think of a sawhorse, or a line of sawhorses joined together*

The Kapellbrücke was built with triangular **trusses** set on piled trestles. A **truss** is a support structure built of straight beams, usually arranged in triangles. Trusses can be built above or below the roadway of a bridge, and we'll talk more about var-ious kinds of truss bridges in Chapter 10.

For now it's enough to know that a good part of the Kapell-brücke's supporting structure consists of the triangular roof beams, which give the bridge stability. In the 17th century, the town fathers invited a local painter named Hans Heinrich Wägman to decorate the bridge with paintings. The paintings depict the history and mythology of the city. Workmen mounted the triangular paintings in the protected space under the roof, within the truss frame. Unfortunately, following a damaging fire in 1993, only thirty of the original 158 paintings have been fully restored.

Paintings in the Chapel Bridge

In the middle of the bridge stands an octagonal tower 34 meters (113 ft) tall. The tower has served as a prison, a torture chamber, and a place to store city records. Today, it's a tourist shop.

The Kapellbrücke was originally 270 meters long, but reinforcement of the river banks over the centuries has decreased the length of the current bridge to only 205 meters. Still, it's well worth strolling across this Chapel Bridge, the oldest covered wooden bridge and oldest truss bridge still standing in Europe.

Mathematical Bridge, Cambridge

Our next bridge is also a pedestrian bridge. This one is quite short and not covered. It's the so-called Mathematical Bridge connecting two parts of Queens' College by crossing the river Cam in Cambridge, England.

Rumor states that the bridge was designed by Sir Isaac Newton without nuts or bolts, but no part of the rumor is true. Newton died in 1727, while the bridge wasn't constructed until 1749. William Etheridge, a master carpenter and civil engineer who had built other bridges, designed the Mathematical

Bridge. James Essex, who also designed many parts of Cambridge's colleges, put it together. And Essex did use bolts to fasten the bridge joints.

So what makes this bridge "mathematical?" If you look closely, you will see that although the bridge has a gradual arch shape overall, no single timber is anything but straight. Eight sets of timbers hold up the bridge. Each supporting timber is set at a tangent to the arch. That is, it brushes against the circle of the arch at just one point. Meanwhile, eight pairs of "vertical" timbers stick straight out from the curve in a radial direction. Between each pair of radial timbers, the bridge arches by $1/32^{nd}$ of a circle, so along its whole eight-pair course it describes one quarter-circle.

Mathematical Bridge, showing tangents

It turns out that this tangent and radial truss structure is quite stable and efficient, without using much timber. People still punt under and walk over the bridge today, almost 300 years after it was built.

Chengyang Bridge 1912

The Dong people are one of 56 ethnic minority groups native to China. They live in a steep, green, mountainous region in Guanxi Province in the southeastern part of the country. So isolated were the Dong people that before 1958 they had no written script for their own language. Eighty percent of Dong land is steep mountainside and ten percent is rivers. Only ten percent is suitable for fields to grow crops. Still, the Dong grow rice, cotton, and timber. They are known for their embroidery and their skillful carpentry. They build their houses on stilts away from the river to avoid flooding and also to preserve space for agricultural land.

To cross rivers, the Dong people build special covered wooden bridges called Wind and Rain bridges. The most famous, crossing between two villages on the Linxi river, is the Chengyang Bridge. Sixty-four meters (210

Chengyang Wind and Rain Bridge

ft) long and 11 meters high, the wooden bridge is set on three stone piers. There are walkways on two levels, with benches along the railings where a person can stop and rest or watch the river. Five roofed pavilions perch atop the bridge, their roofs covered in tile. Each pavilion is "home" to a different deity and includes a shrine and altar. The Chengyang Bridge is much more than a way of crossing a river: it's a religious offering, and for that reason, its builders made it beautiful.

The bridge is constructed of wood in a **cantilever** design. That is, the bridge starts out as a beam cantilever bridge, with one long plank extending out over the gaps separating each pier from the next. Because one plank can't cross the whole gap, another plank, extending farther, is laid on it and pushed farther out.

If you try this yourself, you will see that it's not too many beams (or tongue depressors or popsicle sticks) before your structure collapses. You need to do more.

What helps hold the extended planks in place is the **counterweight** provided by the heavy pavilion structures anchoring one end of the first plank. Meanwhile, another beam extends from the second pier toward the first, until the extended planks meet and can be joined together.

The Dong are such skillful carpenters that they build their wind and rain bridges without any nails, bolts, or metal fastenings. Instead, they use mortise and tenon construction to dovetail the wood, fitting pieces together in a way that keeps them secure by themselves.

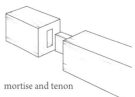

mortise and tenon

Like the Kapellbrücke, the Chengyang Bridge is decorated with art-works. Paintings and carvings line the corridors and eaves. Among them, carved into marble, are the words of the poet Guo Muruo, who so admired the bridge that he composed a poem to honor it.

above: "Chengyang Bridge", calligraphy by Guo Muruo
left: Guo Muruo on his 50th birthday

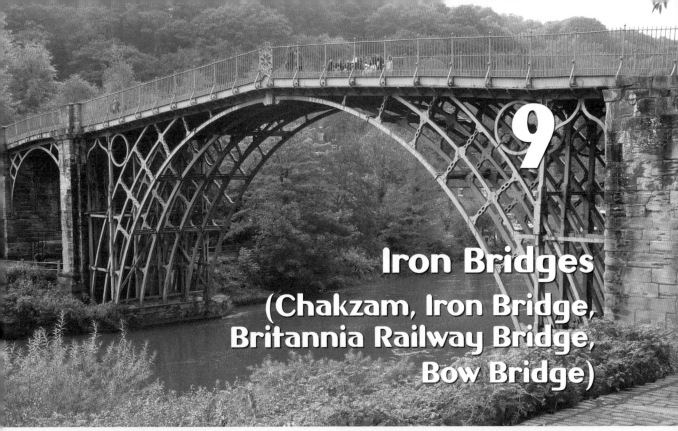

Iron Bridges
(Chakzam, Iron Bridge, Britannia Railway Bridge, Bow Bridge)

Iron Bridge, Shropshire

Thangtong Gyalpo

FOR THOUSANDS OF YEARS, PEOPLE have been heating and melting ore to extract iron to use in making tools or weapons. Eventually, technology improved to the point that iron became a practical, strong material to use in building bridges.

Chakzam Iron Suspension Bridge, Bhutan, 1430

Thangtong Gyalpo was a late medieval Tibetan Buddhist saint who brought iron suspension bridges to the Himalayas. For this contribution, he is often known as Chakzampam, meaning

"Iron Chain Maker." Sometimes people call him King of the Empty Plain or Madman of the Empty Valley.

Thangtong Gyalpo was a master yoga practitioner, religious teacher, and exorcist. At the same time, he practiced the arts of a blacksmith, architect, and engineer. Thangtong was born in 1385 C.E in Tsang, in the Tibetan heartland. After years of study and meditation, he began to travel around today's Tibet and Bhutan to teach Buddhism and build monasteries, stupas and bridges.

Thangtong Gyalpo also created a new art form, the popular Tibetan opera known as *lhamo*. He even formed an opera song and dance troupe of seven sisters to help raise money to buy iron for his great love, bridges. Even today, in Tibetan opera performances, the figure of Thangtong Gyalpo, represented as an old man with a long white beard, sits on a special platform to watch the show.

Stupas are domed Buddhist shrines.

Old Chain-Bridge at Chaksam, 1904 by Edmund Candler

In the 1400s, travel through the Himalayas was blocked by steep, deep river gorges. Thangtong Gyalpo wanted people to be able to travel on Buddhist pilgrimages. His solution was suspension bridges. Early on, he may have used twisted willow branches or yak skins to weave his ropes, but for later bridges he bought iron ore from local people. Thangtong trained his disciples in blacksmithing, showing them how to extract and shape iron. He forged large iron links into chains that he strung across the gorges. His disciples hung wire or yak-hair rope from the chains to support narrow wire walkways.

An analysis of one Thangtong Gyalpo's foot-long chain links, carried out in 1970, found a high concentration of arsenic mixed into the iron. This addition actually made the iron into a form of steel, though at a much lower temperature than would usually be required. A little arsenic in the mix may be what kept the iron from rusting for centuries.

Tradition says the engineer yogi oversaw the building of 58 such bridges in Tibet and Bhutan—along with sixty wooden bridges and 118 ferry crossings. Each crossing had a religious meaning. Buddhism teaches of four stages of change in a person's life: birth, sickness, old age, and death. For the bridge-building monk, every crossing he built represented the way wisdom allows us to pass safely across each stage.

One of the earliest such crossings was a bridge built in 1430 across the Kyichu River in Lhasa. This bridge Thangtong Gyalpo personally planned and supervised. For later bridges, he often entrusted the actual construction to disciples.

Thangtong Gyalpo's most famous bridge, the iron suspension bridge leading to the monastery at Chuwori, broke in 1594. Several pilgrims plummeted to the water below. After repair, the bridge was used regularly for another 280 years. Its remnants were finally destroyed during the Chinese Cultural Revolution, when revolutionary youths sought to wipe out any traces of "backward" religion.

Luckily, arsenic mixed into iron (this happens in modern steel too) does not get absorbed into people's bodies, so there's no chance of poisoning.

Chushul suspension bridge, built 1430, sketched by an Indian spy working for the Survey of India in 1878

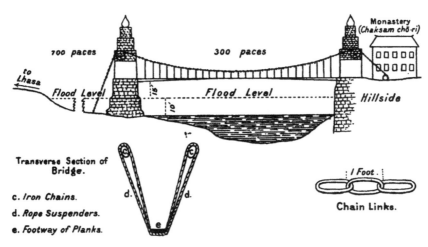

IRON SUSPENSION BRIDGE OVER TSANGPO.

Chakzam bridge in Bhutan

Today, there appear to be several remaining bridges known as the Chakzam Bridge and attributed to Thangtong Gyalpo. The first of them, in Tibet itself, crosses the Yarlung Tsangpo river near Lhasa. Today it is only a remnant—just two chains remain. When the yogi built it in 1430, it had the longest unsupported central span in the world: 137 meters. Two other existing bridges named Chakzam exist in Bhutan and India. Villagers throughout the Himalayan region still use suspension bridges, constructed of iron links, steel cables, and wire.

Iron Bridge, Shropshire, 1781 (cast iron)

The next step in iron bridge design required the use of cast iron. Cast iron is made by melting iron ore in a blast furnace and adding small amounts of carbon and silicon. Because of its relatively low melting point (less than 1200 degrees C), cast iron is good for casting (pouring into a mold) to create specific shapes. Its main downfall is that it is brittle.

Smelting is extracting metal from rock or ore by heating and melting it.

In a Shropshire village named Coalbrookdale, Abraham Darby first smelted local iron ore with carbon from local coal in 1709. This method allowed Darby to produce iron cheaply. Because of Darby's iron, Shropshire became a center for the growing Industrial Revolution. But the Severn River, while useful for boat traffic, made trade across land difficult. People began to ask for a bridge.

In 1773, architect Thomas Farnolls Pritchard wrote to a local ironmaster, John Wilkinson, with a proposal. A cast-iron bridge, he suggested, could cross the river in a single

Iron Bridge

span. Money was raised, and Abraham Darby III, grandson of the first ironmaster, was appointed treasurer.

At first, the men funding the project wavered: should the bridge be built of stone, wood, or iron? They finally settled on iron. A carpenter designed the bridge, which was then manufactured in sections offsite. Nearly 1700 iron components were cast individually and fitted together. Components meant to be identical actually varied by several centimeters in different parts of the bridge. The heaviest component weighed 5.5 tons.

Darby had promised to build the bridge for £3250, so when the cost rose to £6,000, he had to go into debt to bear the difference himself. But once the bridge opened in 1781, tolls flowed in, and by the mid-1790s, the bridge was paying its investors an annual dividend of 8 percent.

A dividend is a percentage of profits paid to every shareholder or part owner of a business.

Later evaluation of the bridge suggested that it was over-built and unnecessarily heavy. Cast iron has remarkable compressive strength but relatively low tensile strength, meaning it is subject to bending or even cracking. Still, during a flood in 1795, the iron bridge was the only Severn bridge not swept away. Its strength protected it, along with the small surface area it presented for high waters to push against.

Repairs over the past 300 years have focused mostly on the wooden and stone components of the bridge. In the 1970s, the road surface was replaced by tarmac. Today, the bridge is used by pedestrians and tourists only, while vehicles travel over a nearby concrete bridge.

Bow Bridge, Central Park, 1862

Bow Bridge was the second cast-iron bridge in America and is the longest bridge in Central Park. It was designed by Calvert Vaux and Jacob Wrey Mould as part of the great landscape architect Frederick Law Olmstead's overall plan for pathways meandering through the park. Constructed between 1859 and 1862, the light and airy Iron Bridge is meant for walkers. Its 60-foot span crosses The Lake from Cherry Hill to the Ramble. Playful circles decorate the bridge's sides and reflect in calm water below. The walkway is made of a very hard South American wood called ipe, which turns reddish when wet. Especially in fall, the colors of the walkway, the changing leaves, and the white of the bridge make a striking contrast.

Bridges in films can stand for all sorts of concepts, such as reaching across divisions between people or transitioning to a new phase of life. Of course, sometimes, a bridge just provides a beautiful setting.

The Bow Bridge is a favorite setting for romantic movies set in New York City, including *Manhattan, The Way We Were, Glee, Spiderman 3, Night at the Museum*, and more. Visitors love to fish off the bridge or row beneath it in a rented boat.

Britannia Railway Bridge, Wales, 1850 (wrought iron)

By 1960, there were 60,000 railway bridges in Britain!

In the mid 1800s, railways spread across Britain. With them came the need for more and stronger bridges. Most existing bridges, though they could stand up to horse and carriage traffic, would buckle under a roaring locomotive weighing several tons. To meet the demand of the railroads, the new bridges had to be built quickly. Materials used included wood, masonry (stone or brick) and, more and more often, iron.

Robert Stephenson

Every new engineering project has to overcome certain challenges or **constraints**—conditions that have to be met. For bridges, constraints include location, local rules, available materials, expected load, time, and money.

Britannia Tubular Bridge, over the Menai Straits, shewing the float by Hawkins, G., 1850

The requirements sound impossible. That is what's awesome about bridges: so often, they require innovation in both materials and design.

In 1848, Robert Stephenson, chief engineer for the Chester and Holyhead Railway, faced the challenge of building a bridge across the Menai strait from Bangor on the mainland of Wales to the island of Anglesey just off the coast. A tiny island mid-stream offered a place to set one tower. But ships navigated through the strait toward the Irish Sea, and the Admiralty decreed that any bridge crossing it would have to leave vertical clearance of at least 31.5 meters above high water. Moreover, the channel could not block shipping while the bridge was being built.

Because towers or piers block shipping, the bridge would need to span great lengths between the planned towers, more than wood could bear. And the Admiralty would not allow the thick piers and immense scaffolding or **falsework** supports necessary for huge stone arches. So Stephenson decided to use wrought iron. Wrought iron is iron that has been worked and beaten into shape, not just cast. It has greater tensile strength than cast iron, meaning it is resistant to stretching, bending and breaking.

In order to create the strongest possible bridge without overwhelming weight, Stephenson decided on a tubular design. The trains would run through what was essentially a long tube open on both ends. After experimenting with circular and oval tubes, Stephenson demonstrated that the strongest option was a four-sided, box-like tube. The sides were built of wrought iron plates. Each side reinforced and stabilized the other three. Running under the bottom surface of the box were iron beams that themselves were long, hollow boxes—**box girders**.

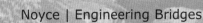

We'll talk more about box girders in Chapter 11.

In a further innovation, Stephenson insisted on testing scale models of his bridge to make sure it would be strong enough to bear a live load of locomotives. He went so far as to build a one-sixth scale model, which stood up to a load of 86 tons before it failed.

Stephenson's team built five masonry towers—a central one rooted on the small mid-channel Britannia Rock, one in the water on either side, and two serving as abutments or anchoring structures on the two shores. These monumental towers rose as high as 70 meters (230 feet) above their foundations. In fact, they loomed high above the railway deck itself. This extra height was unnecessary. Stephenson designed it in part so the towers would look magnificent. But he did so also to pacify doubters. If someone later decided the bridge deck needed extra support, cables could be strung from the towers. This never happened.

For the shore-side sections of the bridge, workers riveted iron tubes into place over timber scaffolding. But the Admiralty would not allow the strait itself to be blocked during construction, so Stephenson had to come up with a unique solution.

He directed each of the three central towers to be built with niches at water level and long vertical grooves extending all the way from the water to the height of the bridge deck. In June 1849, a section of tube was carried by barge and fitted at high tide into the niches and then the grooves of the first two towers. A huge hydraulic lift then slid the iron section, 144 meters in length, up the grooves and into place. Masons promptly filled in the grooves in the towers below the iron section so it couldn't slide back down. Then the team moved on to use their lifting method for the next span. Once all the pieces were aligned, the bridge was fitted together. Stephenson himself drove the very last of its two million rivets.

When the heaviest trains crossed the bridge, Stephenson measured its deflection. The bridge bent by a distance of less than two inches. Wrought iron had proved its tensile strength.

The Britannia Bridge stayed in use for 120 years. Stone lions guarded its entrances. In 1970, a group of people exploring the tube lit some paper to see it better. As their fire blazed out of control, the tremendous heat caused the iron tubes to sag and crack. To repair the bridge, engineers reused Stephenson's stone towers, but replaced the old iron tube with a new double-deck structure carrying a road above and rails below. They did so with shallow arches built from the material that has replaced wrought iron worldwide—steel. The arches themselves used trusses, a structure that we will examine in the next chapter.

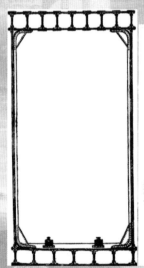

A cross-section of one of the Brittania bridge tubes

Construction of tubes on the Carnarvon shore, 1849

Truss Bridges
(Pont-y-Cafnau, Qiantang River Bridge)

Qiantang River Bridge

Y OU HAVE PROBABLY SEEN BRIDGES WITH LOTS OF straight lengths of wood or metal crisscrossing above or below the deck. These are truss bridges. They came into common use in the 1800s, especially for railroad bridges, and they are still important today.

Triangles are the most stable geometric forms. They are the most difficult to bend or pull out of shape. You can try this yourself. Tack three straws together in a triangle, and four straws together in a square. If you press on one corner of your structure, which one is easier to push out of shape?

A truss is a structure or framework that bears weight and holds itself together. Most often it is built of straight components arranged in triangles. A truss is designed to distribute and balance the forces of tension and compression, pulls and pushes.

Early truss bridges were built of wood, especially in America, where pine forests were plentiful. Later, iron and then steel replaced wood. Today, some truss bridges are built of reinforced concrete.

A basic element of many truss bridges is the king-post truss. Think of a weight bearing down on the top of a triangle. The force is carried down the two diagonal segments. It tends to push the two bottom ends apart, but in a king truss these ends are held together by a horizontal segment. A "king post "or vertical piece runs from the top of the triangle to the middle of the bottom horizontal piece, helping to hold it in place.

king-post truss

In Roman times and in the Middle Ages, builders used king-post trusses, most often to support roofs. American colonists brought the king-post design with them to the new continent. When they needed to build a bridge across a short span, colonists cut logs and arranged them in supporting triangles, often using a king-post design.

We've already seen one truss bridge in this book. The Mathematical Bridge at Cambridge (Chapter 8, p. 49) is actually a radial and tangent truss arrangement of triangles.

Trusses made sense for wooden bridges made of hewn logs. They made even more sense for iron bridges. Iron is so heavy that the builder needs to cut out any parts of the structure that are not necessary to hold the bridge together. Trusses leave lots of empty space between their components, reducing their overall weight. Let's take a look at a few truss bridges.

The Pont-y-Cafnau in Wales is the oldest surviving iron railway (actually tramway) bridge. Only 47 feet long, it was built in 1793 for the Cyfarthfa Ironworks. The bridge enabled workmen to bring in water and tram loads of limestone for the ironworks' blast furnaces. One of the company's partners was a man named Watkin George. Trained as a carpenter, he came up with a simple design for the bridge: two stone abutments with an iron king-post truss between them to support the bridge deck. He joined the iron elements with the mortise and tenon design used in fine carpentry.

Although the Pont-y-Cafnau bridge was very small, it was important as a demonstration of building technique. Today it is still used as a public footbridge along a walking trail.

American Truss Bridges

In the 1800s, American bridge builders began to invent variations on the truss theme. The first of them to patent his ideas was the architect Ithiel Town, who in 1820 received a patent for a lattice truss. A lattice is a criss-crossing arrangement of strips of wood or metal. The Town truss had two important ad-

Town lattice

vantages: it could be built by unskilled laborers, and it didn't require massive beams of wood. Town trusses spread across the world, making Ithiel a wealthy man.

It seemed every builder wanted to invent a new kind of truss to name after himself. Here are a few of them!

Warren quadrangular or lattice truss

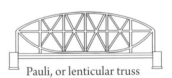
Pauli, or lenticular truss

Warren truss

Pratt truss

As railroads spread across the continent, demand for inexpensive, easy-to-build bridges multiplied. Builders experimented with a variety of truss designs. These included the Bollman, Fink, Whipple, lenticular, Kellogg, Pegram, Schwedler, Pratt, Petit, Howe, and Warren designs. Over time, wrought iron and eventually steel replaced wood as the most common building material.

Still, many of the trusses trembled and shook under the weight of the trains crossing their decks. The most fragile-looking were trestle bridges—high bridges set on delicate-looking towers of timbers or iron bars arranged in crossing patterns. Trestles were common not only in the United States but also in Australia and Canada.

trestle bridge

In 2006, somebody counted 446 bridges in Pittsburgh! Can you find 15 of them in this aerial photo?

Qiantang River Bridge

Pittsburgh, where the young Chinese engineer Mao Yisheng studied bridge design, boasts three major rivers surrounded by hills. It is known as the City of Bridges. Most are truss bridges.

Returning to China in 1919, Mao took the idea of truss bridges with him. Fourteen years later, when the authorities asked him to build a bridge to cross the Qiantang River, he turned to trusses for a strong, affordable design.

The Qiantang River passes through the city of Hangzhou in eastern China. More than 1,500 years ago during the Sui dynasty, Chinese engineers connected Hangzhou to Beijing via the Grand Canal. The canal allowed trade to flourish, and Hangzhou became a beautiful and prosperous city.

The world's first known tide table—predicting when high and low tides would occur—was written for the Qiantang River at Hangzhou in 1056. It was needed because the tides at Hangzhou are high and fierce. At certain times of the month, when tidal waters pile up in Hangzhou Bay and funnel into the river mouth, a roaring wave of tidal salt water surges up the river. Chinese people call it the "Silver Dragon." Surfers come from all over the world to ride the dragon. In 2007, two surfers from France and Brazil rode a single wave up the river for 17 kilometers!

With such tidal surges, building a bridge over the Qiantang presented a huge challenge. Mao's design called for a double-decker bridge carrying both a highway and a railroad. The bridge was 1,453 meters (4,767 ft) long with 16 spans between stone piers. The English company Dorman Long pre-built steel sections with a Warren truss design. At a time of quiet tide, these sections were floated to the correct space, lifted into place and connected with steel rivets. The bridge opened to traffic on September 26, 1937. It was the first double-decked steel bridge in China, and the first modern bridge to be designed by a Chinese engineer.

But Mao's chance to celebrate was brief. In November of 1937, the invading Japanese army took over the port city of Shanghai and launched an assault on Hangzhou. To help defend the city, the young engineer, following orders, used explosives to destroy his new bridge. It had stood for only 89 days.

After the war ended, Mao Yisheng oversaw the effort to rebuild the bridge. But China had a lot of reconstruction to do, and the bridge had to wait its turn. It was not until 1953 that the Qiantang River bridge reopened to traffic.

Truss bridges continue to be built today, especially over relatively short spans.

11

First Steel Bridge – The Eads Bridge Over The Mississippi

IRON BRIDGES HADN'T BEEN AROUND LONG BEFORE THEY gave way to steel bridges. In the last chapter, you already saw one such bridge, the Qiantang River Bridge. In next two chapters, we'll go back to see the earliest steel bridges, and how they opened a whole new era in bridge engineering.

The difference between iron and steel can be confusing. Iron is an element, number 26 on the periodic table. Steel is a mixture of iron and other elements. Steel contains about 2% carbon, which is less carbon than cast iron but more than wrought iron. It can also include small amounts of other metals and semi-metals, like chromium (in stainless steel), silicon, tungsten, manganese and more. Different elements added to steel give it slightly different properties, such as increased hardness or resistance to corrosion. Generally, steel is stronger and less brittle than iron.

The first great pioneer in steel bridge building, and the first American civil engineer to become known around the world, was a self-taught engineer named James Buchanan Eads. Born in 1820, Eads was named after his cousin James Buchanan, who later became fifteenth president of the United States.

Living in St. Louis, Missouri, Eads grew up poor. His father abandoned the family when James was thirteen, so the boy left school to help support his mother and sisters by selling apples on the street. Soon he found work in a general store, where he spent his free time reading books about physics and machinery. Hoping to earn money for marriage, he started a glassworks, but the business failed. He fell deeply into debt.

At age twenty-two, Eads came up with an idea for salvaging wrecks from the Mississippi River. There was money to be made recovering materials from sunken riverboats, and when Eads showed his design for a salvage vessel to a pair of shipbuilders, they decided to back him financially.

To aid in his salvage work, Eads eventually built ten boats from which he lowered diving bells of his own invention. Each diving bell was a wine barrel open at the bottom but weighted enough that it sank to the riverbed even though it was filled with air. Inside the bell, a diver—often Eads himself—could walk the bottom or explore the decks of a drowned vessel. His third salvage vessel was strong and heavy enough that it could even pump air into a sunken wreck and raise it entirely from the deep.

Eads began to make money. When the Civil War started, he was a wealthy man, recognized as an expert on the Mississippi River. A patriot, he proposed building ironclad riverboats to defend the great river. Eads eventually built thirty vessels for the Union, employing 4000 men in shifts day and night.

When the war ended, the leadership of St. Louis contemplated a grand new project. St. Louis had grown and thrived because of riverboat traffic along the Mississippi, but by the late 1860s, steamboats weren't enough. A

James B. Eads

Those who make their living transporting people and good by water often oppose new bridges—not only because a bridge might get in their way but because they don't welcome the competition!

network of railroads spanned the country like a spiderweb, and more and more trade goods traveled by rail. St. Louis merchants and bankers wanted their city to be a crossroads for this traffic, but the turbulent Mississippi presented a barrier. So the city fathers invited proposals for a bridge to carry both vehicles and trains across the Mississippi.

The challenges were daunting. The river current was strong. In winter, ice floes battered the banks. Moreover, riverboat captains, who didn't want a bridge siphoning off any of their business, insisted on a set of seemingly impossible requirements. The bridge had to be high enough to let full-sized riverboats pass beneath. No suspension bridge or drawbridge was allowed. No more than two piers could interrupt the river's flow. And during the bridge's construction, river traffic must not be blocked by falsework from below.

Eads submitted a proposal for a high, cantilevered, steel bridge of three arches. It would be the largest steel structure ever built. When some officials fretted that his design would be too difficult to build, Eads replied, "Must we admit that, because a thing has never been done, it never can be, when our knowledge and judgment assures us it is entirely practical?" He won the contract.

Eads designed the bridge to consist of hollow steel tubes 18 inches in diameter. These tubes would be built into a pattern of supporting triangles and laid across two huge stone piers set in the river. The greatest challenge Eads faced led to an innovation that revolutionized bridge building. For the foundation of each of two massive stone piers, he had to dig a gigantic hole underwater. The foundation had to reach one hundred feet through Mississippi mud to reach the bedrock below.

His solution, a caisson, was a heavy, watertight wooden room, open at the bottom like one of his diving bells, that could be lowered to the riverbed. A passageway extended from the caisson through its roof to the water's surface; a ladder allowed workmen to climb in and out. Men working inside, on the caisson's open floor, dug stones and mud from the river bottom. They fed this loosened material into a vacuum system that spewed it out the top.

Air inside the caisson had to be pressurized to hold back the mud and water above. The deeper the caissons sank into the mud, the higher the air pressure had to be inside them. Soon men who emerged from working below began to show symptoms of an unknown new affliction—caisson disease. On their way home from work, these men staggered with sudden joint pains or even collapsed.

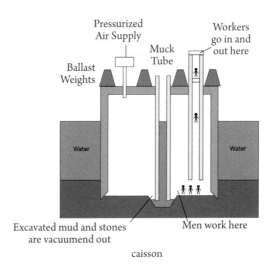

caisson

Today we would recognize caisson disease as decompression sickness or "the bends." The same sickness affects scuba divers who surface too rapidly. When people breathe air under high pressure, some of the nitrogen gas in the air dissolves in their blood. If scuba divers surface too fast or workers climb too quickly out of an underground chamber, the nitrogen gas comes out of solution and forms bubbles in their blood, just as carbon dioxide forms bubbles in a soft drink when you pop open the can. These bubbles block blood flow to muscles, joints, or even the brain. Tissue dies for lack of oxygen. The result can be painful or crippling.

Nobody at the time knew what caused caisson disease, but Eads limited how long his workers remained below. He cut their alcohol intake and saw that they got good nutrition. He even built a floating hospital on the river to care for injured men. Still, over the course of the seven years it took to build the bridge, fifteen men died of caisson disease, and scores of others were seriously injured.

Once the foundation piers were built up from bedrock, Eads used a cantilever building method. No supporting falsework underneath blocked river traffic. A system of cables passed from a fixed anchorage point on either shore, across wooden towers built atop the piers. These cables held up the free ends of pre-built tubular steel arches. Each arch had one end resting on shore and the other end suspended in air until the cables lowered it into place. A threaded plug of wrought iron then screwed the two ends of the bridge together.

In 1874, after seven years and nearly ten million dollars spent on its construction, the bridge was complete. To prove to the public that it was safe and sturdy, Eads had an elephant walk across it. Then he directed 26 locomotives to cross at the same time. The bridge held. The official opening day on July 4, 1874, featured a parade fifteen miles long.

People believed that an elephant would refuse to step on unsteady ground.

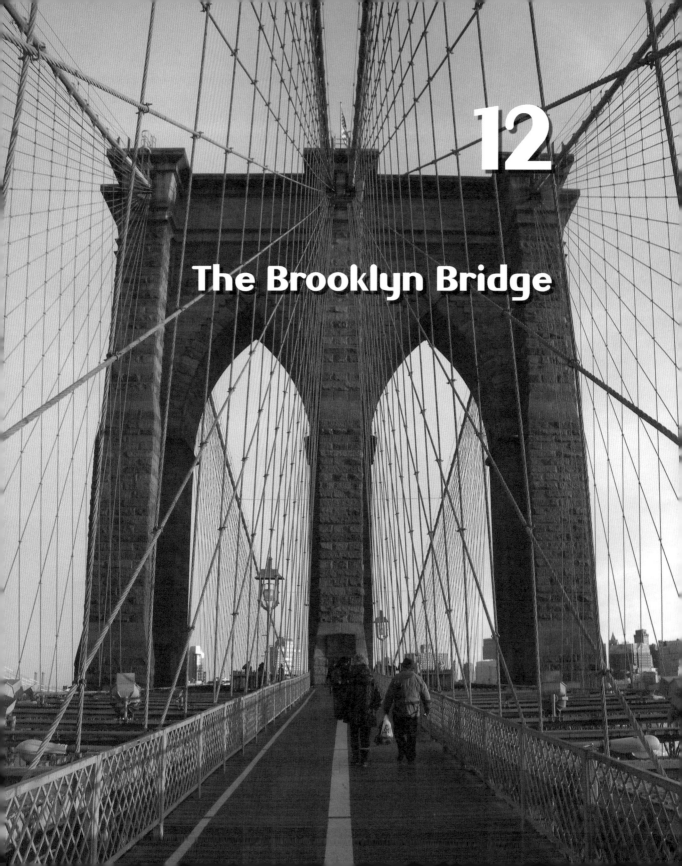

12

The Brooklyn Bridge

T HE NEXT GREAT STEEL BRIDGE BEGAN CONSTRUCTION only two years after the Eads bridge. For decades, New Yorkers had thought about ways to connect Manhattan with Brooklyn, a growing city just across the East River. Engineers debated whether a tunnel or a bridge would be more practical. A German immigrant named John Augustus Roebling (born 1806) advocated for a massive bridge that would symbolize the power and hope of America.

John Augustus Roebling

Roebling had studied architecture and engineering in Germany before emigrating to America as a young man. He tried his hand at farming in Pennsylvania, but soon moved to New Jersey, where he started a business manufacturing steel "wire rope." He grew interested in the new science of building suspension bridges, where the roadbed was supported by wires hanging from cables slung across a gap. The Inca bridges were rope suspension bridges, but Roebling, like Eads, wanted to use steel.

Suspension bridges earned a bad name for themselves in the mid 1800s, because they kept falling down. The Angers Bridge in France, the Wheeling suspension bridge in West Virginia, and four suspension bridges built by one Samuel Brown, all came down—under marching troops or battered by high winds. Usually the cause was torsion. Unlike Inca rope bridges, which could freely twist in the wind, 19th century suspension bridges had stiff decks for vehicles. If high winds or the rhythmic tramp of marching troops caused the bridge to sway and twist, the stiff deck often cracked and gave way.

Roebling's solution was to add cross cables that stiffened the bridge deck further, preventing it from waving or twisting. His approach later became common in what was known as cable-stayed bridges. Roebling built suspension aqueducts and then railroad bridges, including one in Pittsburgh, one across the Ohio River at Cincinnati, and finally a magnificent span across the Niagara River below the falls.

But Roebling's grandest dream was to build a bridge across New York's East River. For more than fifteen years, he worked to persuade local politicians that his design would work.

Roebling's plan centered on two massive neo-Gothic (pointed arch) towers built of limestone and granite. By height and overall mass, they would be the largest structures anywhere in the Americas. Four suspension cables of twisted steel fiber would pass from anchorage buildings, one in Brooklyn and one in Manhattan, across the top of the towers. Vertical wires hanging from the cables would support two decks for rail and vehicle traffic. Slanting stays would stabilize the decks to keep them from twisting in the wind. In 1867, the New York state legislature approved the idea, and a bridge company was formed.

Two years later, with construction finally about to start, Roebling was standing on a jetty taking final compass readings. A ferry boat, lurching against the pier, crushed his right foot. Roebling's toes had to be amputated. Roebling bore the amputation without anesthesia, but then tetanus set in. His muscles went into painful spasms. Three weeks later, the master engineer was dead.

Responsibility for the bridge fell to his thirty-two-year-old son, Washington Roebling, himself a trained engineer. The younger Roebling set to work, faithfully following his father's plans. As with the Eads bridge, an early task was to build stone piers mid-river. Washington Roebling had studied the use of caissons in Europe, and he devised refinements of his own. Soon teams of men were working in darkened rooms deep beneath the tidal waters of the East River. Each wooden caisson, built of yellow pine, had a floor area the size of four tennis courts. After careful testing, Roebling allowed not only digging but blasting at the floor of the caissons. Progress was slow, but the caissons inched deeper.

The dark working space inside the caissons was lit by burning lamps, creating a constant risk of fire. In December 1870, a serious conflagration broke out in the caisson at the Brooklyn end of the bridge. Working its way into the ceiling timbers, the fire threatened the entire caisson with collapse. The men inside, at risk of drowning, fought the fire with drills and jets of water. Roebling himself worked underground for so many hours that on his way home afterward he collapsed with exhaustion and caisson disease.

Brooklyn Bridge by Joseph Stella

For a while he was unable to stand or walk. In the end, workers had to completely flood the caisson to extinguish the smoldering blaze.

Later, after many more weeks of work beneath the river, Roebling's health broke down entirely. Unable to read, walk any distance, or tolerate crowds, Washington Roebling oversaw the final eleven years of bridge construction through a telescope from the upper story of his nearby Brooklyn home. He dictated detailed instructions to his wife, Emily Warren Roebling, who corresponded with the assistant engineers and the oversight board.

Emily grew so knowledgeable about mathematics and construction that some newspapers claimed she was the true chief engineer.

Construction of the Brooklyn Bridge was finally completed in 1883, fourteen years after it began, at a total cost of $15.5 million and twenty-seven lives. Its longest span was 1595.5 feet. President Chester A. Arthur attended the opening day ceremony. The first person to ride across the finished bridge was Emily Warren Roebling, holding a rooster, symbol of victory, in her lap, while her husband watched through his telescope. Following her that first day came 150,000 people, riding in horse-drawn vehicles or strolling on the pedestrian walkway above the vehicle roadway. When evening came, a fireworks display lit the bridge, and gunfire boomed from ships passing below.

Six days later, a woman spectator jostled by the crowd of spectators fell down a set of stairs. Panicked sightseers stampeded. Twelve people were crushed to death. Still, the bridge remained a popular tourist destination. Newspapers dubbed it "The Eighth Wonder of the World." Poets wrote about it and artists painted it. Trains crossed. Daredevils jumped from it—perhaps half of them survived. As Brooklyn grew, more bridges and tunnels across the East River followed, but the Brooklyn Bridge remained a prominent symbol of wealth, progress, and power, just as John Augustus Roebling had imagined.

Brooklyn Bridge and Manhattan Bridge in the East River

13
Beams And Girders

A BEAM OR GIRDER BRIDGE IS THE SIMPLEST AND OLDEST of all bridges. Throw a log across a stream and you have a beam bridge. Its major component is a stiff horizontal piece supported at its two ends.

Girders are long beams. Often made of concrete or steel instead of wood, girders are usually directed along the length of the bridge. In a steel girder bridge, the main long pieces will be called girders, while cross pieces may be referred to as steel beams.

When a load sits on top, a beam or girder transfers the load to the supports at its ends. Still, the middle of the beam is subjected to stress, both compression and tension. The longer the beam, the more likely it is to break in the middle. The stronger and taller the beam, the better it resists the stress. To build a safe girder bridge, engineers have to balance the span, height, and strength of the girders.

Most steel or concrete girders rely on a basic shape called an I-beam. From the end, the beam looks like a capital I. The wide flanges at the top and bottom carry the load, while the tall middle part, or web, transfers force downward and then sideways to the bridge piers.

To manufacture small steel girders, steelworkers feed metal stock through pairs of rollers that squeeze them into a uniform shape and thickness. Larger girders use steel plates, which generally consist of I-beams bolted, riveted, or welded together.

The first plate girder bridge was actually made of wrought iron and built for the Baltimore and Oriole Railroad in 1847. Plate girder bridges are usually adequate to carry trains or traffic for relatively short spans. An optimum depth-to-length ratio is about 1:12. Thus, a bridge 24 meters long would have to rest on I-beams two meters high. Vertical stiffeners may have to be added to support the I-beams in the middle of the span.

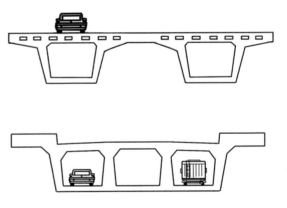

I-beam

Box girders are long hollow boxes. In cross section, a box girder has the shape of a rectangle or a trapezoid. Because it has two sides, or webs, a box girder can support a heavier load than an I-beam. It is also better at resisting torsion, or twisting. And of course, it is much lighter than a solid beam of the same height and width.

Usually, box girders lie under the bridge deck and support it. But sometimes, the road or railway runs right through the center of the box. One example is the Britannia Railway Bridge discussed in Chapter 9, page 52. Here the railway passes through the length of the box girder; such a girder is often called a tubular girder.

When box girders are made of steel, they are usually manufactured off-site and lifted into place by cranes. Concrete girders may be manufactured off-site or cast in place over falsework supports.

Between the bridge superstructure and the piers of a girder bridge, as in other bridges, there are bridge bearings. You can get a glimpse of these when you pass under a highway bridge. Usually, the wide top surface of the pier is not all in contact with the bridge deck. Instead, some smaller piece intervenes. Bearings allow a certain amount of movement between the deck and the pier. This means the bridge can bend slightly under the weight of traffic or shift slightly in case of an earthquake without breaking.

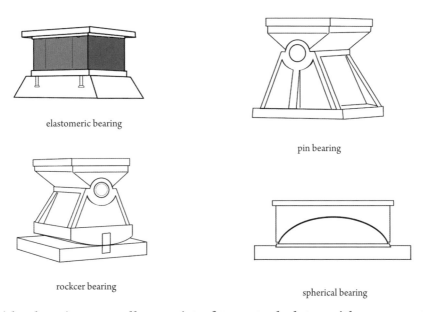

elastomeric bearing

pin bearing

rockcer bearing

spherical bearing

Bridge bearings usually consist of two steel plates with some material between them. Depending on how they are attached, the steel plates may allow the bridge deck to rock, slide, roll, or rotate on the pier. For protection against earthquakes, the middle layer of a bearing may be made of a rubber product. The rubber can absorb and dampen shaking forces.

Beam or girder bridges are not always the most beautiful bridges, but they are the most common ones. Highway bridges and overpasses, many footbridges, and short railway bridges are likely to be beam or girder bridges. While not as long as suspension bridges, they can reach spans of over 300 meters.

The official name is the President Costa e Silva Bridge.

One example is Brazil's Rio-Niterói Bridge across Guanabara Bay in Rio de Janeiro. When the bridge was completed in 1974, it was the second longest bridge in the world. Today, it is still the longest prestressed concrete bridge in the southern hemisphere. Built with a box girder construction, the bridge is 13.29 kilometers (8.26 miles) long. Its center span is 300 meters long, the third longest girder in the world. With a height of 73 meters, the bridge allows hundreds of ships to pass beneath it every month, while 140,000 vehicles cross over it each day.

Rio-Niterói Bridge

In the late 1960s and early 1970s, a series of steel box girder bridges failed under construction. In 1969, temperature expansion and shrinkage led to the sudden failure of a bridge over the Danube in West Germany. Three loud bangs sounded, and the free end of the bridge suddenly swung downward, hanging loose like an elephant's trunk. Luckily, no one was killed.

Seven months later, workers were constructing a seven-span box girder bridge over the River Cleddau in Wales. A free end of the bridge extended

61 meters out over the river when it suddenly buckled and collapsed, killing four men.

In 1971, a similar bridge was under construction in West Germany. This bridge, too, buckled and hung into the water like a giraffe taking a drink. Thirteen people were killed. A few months later, a box girder bridge failed in East Germany, killing four more people. Communist East Germany covered up news of the accident.

The greatest blow came in 1970, from the West Gate Bridge in Melbourne, Australia. This bridge was to be eight lanes wide, with five spans crossing a total length of 848 meters. The contractor built each span in two halves, planning to lift them into place with cranes. But one of the half-spans, when lifted, buckled a bit. In the air, workers removed some bolts, slid one flange over another, and flattened out the buckle. Then, they lifted the second half into place—but its free end was too high to match the other side.

Workers solved this new problem by adding concrete blocks to the free end to weigh it down. That made the second piece buckle also. When the workmen removed bolts to fix the problem as they had on the other side, the weighed-down bridge section could no longer hold. Its remaining bolts sheared off. The section fell, pulling the partly-connected other half-section with it. Men working inside fell 50 meters to the water and Yarra River mud below. Many other workers were taking a lunch break inside or near construction huts under the bridge when the giant steel structure fell on them. Altogether, 35 people died.

Collapse of the West Gate Bridge

After this series of accidents, construction was stopped on box girder bridges worldwide until engineers could figure out the problems. A number of existing bridges were strengthened with cross supports. Construction firms also came to understand that in a box girder bridge, parts have to fit together perfectly. Forcing one piece to fit against another weakens the bridge.

In the end, the box girder design, because it was lighter than a series of I-beams, was too useful to abandon. Today, girders are often built from pre-stressed concrete rather than steel. Most highway overpasses you see will be built primarily of concrete girders, whether they use I-beams or box girders.

You'll read all about concrete in chapter 17.

New West Gate Bridge, 2008

14

Movable Bridges
(Queen Emma, Tower Bridge, Cape Cod Canal Bridge, Corinth Canal bridges)

Bourne Bridge with Cape Cod Railway Lift Bridge behind

WHEREVER BRIDGES CROSS WATER, TRAVELERS BY LAND cross paths with those who travel by water. In designing such bridges, civil engineers face the problem of how not to block water traffic. The usual solution is to build bridges high enough that ships can pass beneath. But there is another solution: bridges that temporarily move out of the way.

The first movable bridges— drawbridges— were designed to stop traffic, not help it along,

Drawbridges over moats around medieval castles were the first movable bridges. When an enemy approached, defenders inside the front gate turned a windlass, drawing on chains attached to the far end of the drawbridge until the span leaned vertically against the gate. The invaders were left outside the moat.

Today there are bridges that rise, fold, swivel, sink, or tilt. Here are a few of them.

Queen Emma Bridge, Willemstad, Curaçao, 1888, swing bridge

Curaçao, a Caribbean island in the Lesser Antilles not far from the coast of Venezuela, is a former Dutch colony with a population of about 160,000. One story relates that Portuguese sailors named it the Isla de Curaçaon (Isle of Curing), because dying sailors who were left there experienced miraculous cures. Probably these sailors were suffering from scurvy after long ocean crossings, and they healed themselves by eating fresh fruit rich in Vitamin C.

In the 1880s, people of Willemstad, the capital of Curaçao, decided they needed to connect the two sides of the city, Punta and Otrabanda, with a pedestrian bridge across St. Anna Bay. But ship traffic entering the bay was also important. A high bridge was impossible, because lovely, pastel-colored colonial buildings on the Punta side crowded so close to the shore that there was no room to build a large abutment.

The citizens of Curaçao came up with a surprisingly simple solution. They built a wood-planked roadway across 16 permanent pontoon boats, making the Queen Emma the largest non-military pontoon bridge in the world. Better yet, they made the bridge able to swing open. It is still in use today.

A pivot or hinge is located at one end of the bridge. At the opposite end perches a small wooden shelter. Sitting inside, the bridge operator controls a pair of diesel engines whose propellers are set perpendicular to the roadway. When a ship needs to pass, the gatehouse operator sounds a horn. Pedestrians scurry off the bridge. The operator starts up the diesel engines,

and the free end of the bridge begins a long, curving arc toward shore. The entire bridge, pontoon boats and all, swings around until it lies alongside the bank near the feet of the picturesque buildings. The ship passes, the operator reverses the motors, and the bridge swings back into place.

The Queen Emma Bridge works so well, in part, because the waters of St. Anna Bay are usually calm. Today, the harbor at Willemstad welcomes cargo ships and cruise ships alike. The citizens of Willemstad like to call their special bridge, with its low profile and pedestrian-friendly setup, the Swinging Old Lady of Curaçao.

Tower Bridge, London, 1894, bascule bridge

Starting in the 1860s, Londoners began to demand a new bridge in the East End of London. The existing London Bridge was getting too much traffic, both too many pedestrians and too many carts and carriages. But any new bridge had to be high enough to let tall-masted ships pass beneath it.

To design the bridge, engineer John Wolfe-Barry teamed up with architect Sir Horace Jones. Jones wanted to echo the style of the nearby Tower of London, so he planned heavy, steel-framed towers faced with stone. He supported the side spans leading from the shores to these towers with heavy suspension chains. The center span between the towers was a bascule with two leaves. That is, each side could be raised like a drawbridge with the help of a counterweight at the tower end.

For the Tower Bridge, counterweights weighing 2,500 metric tons (a metric ton weighs 2,200 pounds) descend into underground bascule chambers. Giant hydraulic engines located in the base of the bridge's towers provide the extra power needed, along with the counterweights, to hoist the bascules. At one time, eighty people worked to shovel coal and maintain the steam engines needed to raise and lower the bascules up to thirty times a day. Then, in 1976, bridge operators switched to electric power.

Counterweights are also used to raise or lower elevators. In an elevator, a cable passes over a pulley from the elevator to a counter-weight that weighs about the same. The entire system is nearly in balance, so only a little force must be applied to make the elevator move.

Nowadays, Tower Bridge is raised about one hundred time a month. Raising it takes only a minute, but ships may pass slowly beneath, so pedestrians in a hurry can climb up inside the towers to cross a footbridge at the highest level.

Today, concerts are sometimes played inside the bascule chambers underground. During the day, visitors to Tower Bridge can view London from the raised walkway or visit the Victorian museum below. Tourists make sure to dodge the counterweights as they descend.

Cape Cod Canal Bridge, 1935, lift bridge

Less common than bascule or drawbridges are vertical lift bridges. One that can still be found today is the Cape Cod Canal Bridge in Barnstable, Massachusetts. Cape Cod projects like a hitchhiker's thumb from the rectangular main body of Massachusetts. On the Cape's northern side is Cape Cod Bay, and Buzzard's Bay lies to the south. Close to the base of the hitchhiker's thumb, where Cape Cod joins the rest of Massachusetts, a series of tidal

Location of the Cape Cod Canal Bridge

rivers create a waterway that was almost navigable even when the Pilgrims landed. For almost three centuries thereafter, planners, including George Washington, ordered surveys and considered building a canal. But nothing happened until 1909, when the private Cape Cod and New York Canal Company started dredging.

The company charged tolls to passing ships and boats but didn't make as much money as expected. Eventually, the U.S. government purchased the canal. The U.S. Army Corps of Engineers deepened it and stopped charging tolls. Today, along with shipping, dolphins and endangered right whales use the canal for a shortcut.

Then in 1939, at the height of the Great Depression, the Corps of Engineers decided to rebuild an old bridge across the canal. The final design called for a bridge whose deck could lift vertically out of the way of canal traffic. The project employed thousands of unskilled men who would otherwise have no jobs.

The main, lifting span of the new Cape Cod Canal Bridge is 166 meters (544 feet) long. Each end has a counterweight of 1000 tonnes. The span, when lifted, rises to a height of 41 meters, allowing ships to pass easily beneath. At the time it was built, the Cape Cod Canal Bridge was the longest vertical lift bridge in the world.

Corinth Canal, Greece, 1988, submersible

The Corinth Canal in Greece has two submersible bridges—bridges that actually sink straight down into the water. They come to rest eight meters below the surface. Their advantage is that there is no height limit for passing ships. On the other hand, the draft, or depth, of the ships cannot be more than eight meters. Because the canal is narrow, it can be used only in one direction at a time, mostly by tourist vessels.

Corinth Canal submersible bridge

15

Cantilever Bridges
(Niagara Cantilever Bridge, Forth Railway Bridge, Howrah Bridge)

Forth Railway Bridge

Remember, a cantilever is fixed at one end and projects out over space at the other end.

SUPPOSE YOU WANT TO BUILD A BRIDGE OVER a river or valley. How do you keep your structure from falling down as you build it? You can construct a support from below and remove it once you're finished. Or you can work from each end, carefully balancing two long horizontal piece out across the gap. Usually, the middle span of the bridge rests on the two projecting arms and binds them together. Other times, the two projecting arms meet perfectly. This is cantilever construction, pioneered by Gottfried Heinrich Gerber, who patented his approach in 1866.

In the picture on the next page, you can see that the two rigid ends of the human bridge support the span crossing the middle.

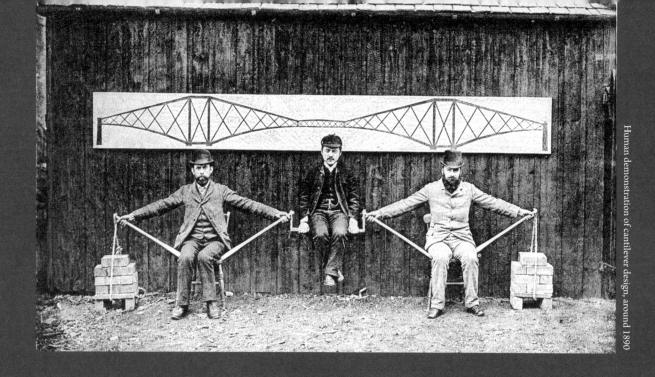

Human demonstration of cantilever design, around 1890

Niagara Cantilever Bridge, Us-Canada border, 1883

In the 19th century, wealthy financier Cornelius Vanderbilt owned several railroads, including the New York Central and Canada Southern Railways. He wanted his own two-lane railway bridge to connect his U.S. and Canadian railway lines. He chose a site in the gorge below Niagara Falls, near the Whirlpool Rapids. In April, 1883, Vanderbilt and his colleagues awarded a contract to engineer Charles Conrad Schneider, who settled on a cantilever design for a bridge made of iron and steel. Vanderbilt challenged Schneider to finish the bridge by November 1—in less than seven months—or pay a fine of $500 per day.

Niagara Railway Bridge

Two iron and steel towers, 45 meters (133 ft) high, were completed October 11. Two cantilevers, each 99 meters long (325 ft) were extended from the towers towards each other. Measuring the space left between them, engineers sent to company headquarters in Buffalo, New York for a center span. Connecting the two cantilever arms, this center section, 37 meters long (120 feet), looked like an ordinary truss bridge.

Newspapers reported the bridge's completion on November 21, 1883, only twenty days late. The first railroad car crossed it, 73 meters (240 feet) above the river, on December 6. The bridge had cost only $700,000. Economical and strong, the Niagara Cantilever Bridge survived heavier and heavier trains for forty years.

Forth Railway Bridge, Scotland, 1890

The Firth of Forth is an estuary gathering up several Scottish rivers and carrying them to the North Sea. In places, the firth is 65 meters deep (220 ft). In the 1880s, railway owners wanted a bridge across it, but the depth made building piers all the way across impractical. Instead, engineers settled on a design based on just three piers—one at each end and a third on a small island in the middle—with cantilever construction in between.

Bridge designers Sir John Fowler and Benjamin Baker erected three steel towers, each set on four circular piers. Because the foundations of these piers had to be set below water level, they used both caissons and cofferdams for the construction.

Once the 100-meter (330 ft) towers were in place, ironworkers built out steel cantilevers. From each tower, workers inched out in both directions simultaneously to keep the structures balanced. They used a truss-like design of strong and rigid steel bars. Altogether, over a period of seven years, 4600 men worked on the bridge. Seventy-three died. Most fell from the structure itself, but others were killed by falling objects, drowning, fire, or caisson disease.

Poet William Morris

When the bridge opened in 1890, it was the longest cantilever bridge in the world: 521 meters (1,709 feet). Its 58,000 tons of steelwork were the heaviest of any structure on earth. Poet William Morris called it "the supremest specimen of all ugliness," but today it is a UNESCO World Heritage Site (see it on page 90), still carrying as many as 200 trains a day.

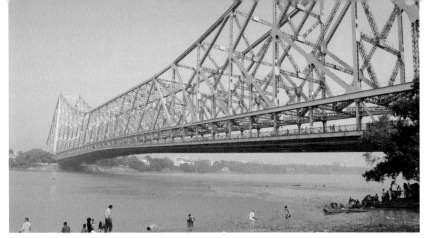

Hooghly River and Howrah Bridge

Howrah Bridge, India, 1942

People once crossed the Hooghly River between the cities of Howrah and Kolkata (Calcutta) on a floating bridge of timber. But by 1936, the bridge was fifty years old and crumbling under the weight of pedestrians, livestock, and vehicles. So engineers designed an immense cantilever bridge with a single span between two towers.

Creeper cranes worked their way out from anchor piers on land to the towers, rising to a height of 82 meters (270 feet) at the river's edge. Each pier required more than 40,000 tons of poured concrete. The cranes crept farther, toward the center of the river. When the two arms were only half a meter (18 inches) apart, workers jacked them together, joining them. Altogether, the bridge used 26,500 tons of steel.

Bridge construction was completed in 1942. By that time, Japan, the U.S., and Britain, which still ruled India, were fighting in World War II. No opening ceremony was held for fear of attracting Japanese bombers.

One unusual feature of the Howrah Bridge is its pedestrian walkways, which in an echo of the overall design, are also cantilevered. Pedestrians don't appear intimidated by their hanging roadway. Today the Howrah Bridge carries the heaviest traffic of any bridge in Asia. Each day, 100,000 vehicles and 150,000 pedestrians use it to cross the Hooghly River.

Little-known fact: The Howrah Bridge faces a unique threat from pedestrians. After chewing certain stimulants mixed with lime, people often spit onto the bridge. This spit, along with bird droppings and acid rain, eats away at the steel. Contractors must continually scrub the bridge clean and add layers of zinc primer and aluminum paint to protect its steel!

Suspension Bridges
(Golden Gate, Akashi Kaikyo)

SUSPENSION BRIDGES LOOK LIGHT AND AIRY. THEY SEEM to swing over wide expanses like trapeze artists. The basic idea of hanging a rope between two points to cross a river has been known for centuries: think of the Inca rope bridges and the chain bridges built by the Tibetan saint Thangtong Gyalpo. Still, it's only in the past century or so that suspension bridges have become an art form of their own.

Today's suspension bridges hang from suspension cables strung over tall towers and anchored at both ends. Between these towers, the cables droop in graceful curves. From points along their length, vertical suspension "ropes" (actually thick wires) hang straight

*The natural curve taken by a rope hanging between two points is called a **catenary**. It depends only on the space between the two points, and it can be described by mathematics.*

down to the bridge decks to hold them up. These vertical suspension wires are part of what differentiates modern suspension bridges from the rope or iron chain bridges of the past. Today, both the massive, curving cables and the suspension wires are usually made of steel.

Golden Gate Bridge, San Francisco, California, 1937

Ask people to think of a bridge, and those who live on the West Coast may well name a particular suspension bridge: the Golden Gate. When it was finished in 1937, the Golden Gate Bridge was the longest and tallest suspension bridge in the world. Until 1964, it could boast the longest main span between two towers. (Today that honor belongs to Japan's Akashi Kaikyo Bridge, described later in this chapter.) Painted a striking reddish orange, the Golden Gate Bridge swoops across the mile-wide opening of San Francisco Bay in three graceful spans. When fog rolls in from the ocean, the bridge seems to float among the clouds.

Before the Golden Gate Bridge, San Francisco's isolation by land slowed its growth. The only way for people to cross from the counties north of San Francisco into the city was by ferry, unless they wanted to drive 160 miles around the bay. The ferry crossing cost only a dollar, but it took time, and by 1930, the ferry docks were choked with waiting traffic.

Bridging the mouth of the bay was thought nearly impossible because of strong tidal currents, fog, and depths of up to 372 feet (113 m) in the middle of the channel. Most engineers believed a bridge would cost far too much to build, perhaps $100 million. But Joseph B. Strauss, a poet as well as a self-taught engineer, devised an idea for a mixed cantilever and suspension bridge that looked like a railroad trestle. Strauss claimed the bridge could be built for just $17 million. In 1919, he submitted his design to the San Francisco city engineer and the mayor. These two sat on the plans for a year before releasing them to the public. The local press called the design ugly. Engineers claimed it would never survive a high wind.

There were other obstacles. U.S. War Department officials originally opposed a bridge across the opening because they worried it would get in the way of tall ships. Furthermore, they feared that if the bridge ever collapsed due to sabotage, war, or accident, the wreckage would block access

to warships and docks in the huge San Francisco harbor. Meanwhile, rail and ferry companies opposed a bridge because they didn't want new-fangled automobiles to poach their passengers. Auto companies, on the other hand, supported the idea.

Still, improved steelmaking was making longer, all-steel suspension bridges possible. A leading New York engineer named Leon Moisseiff published calculations showing that when a thin suspended roadway flexed in the wind, as long as the geometry was right, the forces would be transferred through the vertical suspension wires and curving cables to the towers. This transfer would keep the bridge from collapsing under lateral (sideways) forces.

Bonds are loans to the government from banks or individuals. They play a huge role in funding bridges and other public works projects. In this case, the bonds would be paid off out of income from bridge tolls.

Eventually, the state of California authorized the bridge and issued bonds to pay for it. They appointed Strauss chief engineer while at the same time requiring him to take on a mathematician and engineering professor named Charles Alton Ellis to serve as senior engineer.

Strauss wanted to be seen as the great bridge's primary architect. Ellis, on the other hand, relied heavily on the design ideas of Leon Moussieff. As time passed and costs mounted, Strauss fired Ellis, complaining that he spent too much on telegrams to Moussieff in New York.

Regardless, Ellis remained devoted to the bridge. He continued to work on the mathematics of its design, without pay, for up to 70 hours a week. Today, despite Strauss's efforts to suppress his role, Ellis is recognized as the major designer of the bridge.

The first step in actually constructing the bridge was building the piers for the bridge's two towers. The first pier, on the northern, Marin County side, was straightforward. Bedrock lay only 19.5 feet (6 m) below the surface. Workers used 50,000 tons of concrete strengthened by steel rods to set this tower foundation.

*Remember, a **cofferdam** is an enclosure with walls strong enough to hold back the water, leaving a dry space inside. One advantage of a cofferdam compared to the underwater caissons used in building the Eads bridge and the Brooklyn Bridge is that workers don't labor under high pressure, so they don't suffer from the bends.*

The southern, San Francisco side was much more challenging. The anchoring pier had to be built in 100 feet of water. Strauss and Ellis drove down a steel fender, encased it in concrete, and built it up into a cofferdam that held back the ocean as men worked inside. The southern pier covered the area of a football field filled with concrete.

Take a look at how, in each tower, two parallel posts become slimmer as they rise. Four crossbars attach the posts, with the crossbars coming closer together at higher levels. When seen from below, these design elements exaggerate the viewer's perspective, making the towers look even taller than they are.

Set on these well-founded piers, the Golden Gate's two towers rose to a height of 746 feet above the waves. Built of hollow steel cells riveted together with 1.2 million rivets, the towers were designed to be flexible, strong, and striking. Their style is Art Deco.

Once the towers were complete, machines working their way across the bridge spun the main suspension cables into place. Strauss insisted on rigorous safety standards. He required his workers to wear hardhats on the job, although the hats, like football helmets of the time, were leather. He issued a special hand and face cream to protect workers' skin from the wind, and he recommended a special diet to fight dizziness. Most important, Strauss spent $130,000 on a huge safety net to hang beneath the bridge.

The net caught 19 falling workers over four years. These nineteen called themselves the Halfway to Hell Club. And as a result of the net, the Golden Gate Bridge's excellent safety record—only one death on the job—held nearly to the end. Then, one day in 1937, rivets holding a scaffolding sheared off. Falling, the heavy scaffolding tore through the safety net. Twelve men fell for four seconds, striking the cold, turbulent water at 75 miles per hour. Amazingly, two of the twelve survived.

Each cable of the finished bridge contained 27,572 strands of wire. From the two cables hung 250 pairs of vertical suspension wires to hold up the bridge deck. A slim truss structure, 25 feet (7.6 m) deep, was built under the bridge deck to stiffen and support the roadway. To make sure the bridge would stand out in the fog, workers mixed a bright, orange-red paint, which today is officially called International Orange.

After four years of construction and an expenditure of $27 million, the Golden Gate Bridge was finished. On May 27, 1937, opening day, 200,000 people crossed the bridge on foot or on roller skates. The next day, its six lanes opened to automobile traffic.

 Joseph Strauss wrote a poem to honor the triumph. It begins,

At last the mighty task is done;
Resplendent in the western sun
The Bridge looms mountain high;
Its titan piers grip ocean floor,
Its great steel arms link shore with shore,
Its towers pierce the sky.

Today, 110,000 cars cross the bridge each day. Each day, zipper trucks lay down movable barriers to change the number of lanes open north or south depending on traffic patterns. Strolling pedestrians and pedaling bicyclists on the side walkways enjoy the breeze and the view. On clear days they see the city, Alcatraz, Angel Island, and on the seaward side, the Farallon Islands. Sometimes, migrating gray whales spout in the distance. On foggy days, four huge fog horns on the bridge bellow out a warning to approaching ships. The sound can be heard six miles away.

Two hundred employees, including 38 painters, service the Golden Gate Bridge. Among them, a team of ironworkers are sometimes called on to rescue people who have climbed over a barrier to stand above the ocean, contemplating a jump. It is estimated that 1700 people have committed suicide in the bridge's eighty years. Many more have been talked off the bridge or lifted to safety by bridge workers. In 2018, construction began on a huge, steel suicide prevention net. Colored gray so as not to detract from the bridge's beauty, the net will hang 20 feet below the roadway. Building it will cost $200 million.

In 1989, the Loma Prieta earthquake struck San Francisco with a magnitude of 6.9 on the Richter scale. Although the nearby Bay Bridge partially collapsed, the Golden Gate Bridge survived undamaged. Afterward, engineers analyzed the Golden Gate and found that parts of it might well suffer major damage in a stronger earthquake. Since San Francisco sits on a major fault, the city decided to retrofit the bridge for seismic (earthquake) safety.

The retrofit proceeded over a period of fifteen years. In order to strengthen the bridge without disrupting traffic, engineers built temporary support towers that shouldered the load of the roadway where they worked. They strengthened the tower foundations, joined different truss segments into one continuous truss, and added lateral braces.

At the ends of the bridge, engineers installed seismic expansion joints. These are steel plates where traffic can travel safely, laid over softer, compressible material like silicone foam that can expand or contract under pressure during an earthquake. To the towers, the engineers added isolation bearings, which allow side-to-side movement while absorbing and dampening an earthquake's shaking action.

With these improvements, today's retrofitted Golden Gate bridge is expected to withstand an earthquake of magnitude 8.0 or even higher.

Akashi Kaikyo Bridge, Inland Sea, Japan, 1998

Japan's Akashi Kaikyo Bridge is one part of a remarkable series of bridges that cross between the island of Shikoku and Japan's main island of Honshu. Altogether, three parallel sets of bridges—18 in all—hopscotch across the set of small islands that dot Japan's Inland Sea. Of all those bridges, the Akashi Kaikyo is the longest, tallest, and widest.

The Akashi Kaikyo Bridge is as long as four Brooklyn Bridges laid end to end. The steel wires used in its suspension cables could wrap around the Earth seven and a half times.

Japan suffers downpours, typhoons, earthquakes, and tsunamis—so any Japanese bridge has to be very carefully designed and tested. Undaunted, Japanese engineers planned the longest suspension bridge in the world, with the world's longest central span. To support it, they built steel towers on massive concrete foundations. The towers reach a record 928 feet above the water. A truss underneath the bridge deck provides strength and rigidity while offering little surface area for high winds to batter. In each tower, engineers built in 20 tuned mass dampers. These devices counteract the effects of wind by swinging at the natural resonance frequency of the bridge but in a rhythm and direction opposite to any swinging caused by wind.

At each stage of design, engineers tested a model 1/100th the size of the actual bridge in a wind tunnel. On January 17, 1995, when only the towers were in place, came a real-word test—a massive earthquake measuring 7.1 on the Richter scale. The epicenter of the Kobe earthquake was located deep between the two towers, and the quake moved the towers a whole meter (3.3 feet) farther apart. In the nearby city of Kobe, 4,600 people lost their lives, and across Japan, 400,000 buildings were damaged. But the Akashi Kaikyo towers suffered not one crack.

At the time of the earthquake, the bridge deck connecting the towers had not yet been built. When it came time to add this final piece, engineers used a dual-hinged stiffening girder system. What this means is that the

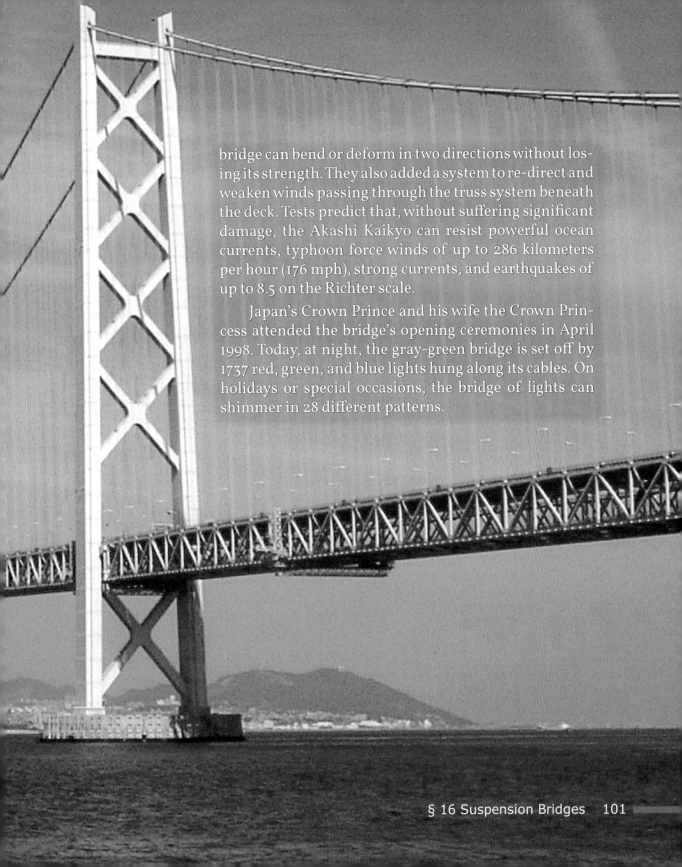

bridge can bend or deform in two directions without losing its strength. They also added a system to re-direct and weaken winds passing through the truss system beneath the deck. Tests predict that, without suffering significant damage, the Akashi Kaikyo can resist powerful ocean currents, typhoon force winds of up to 286 kilometers per hour (176 mph), strong currents, and earthquakes of up to 8.5 on the Richter scale.

Japan's Crown Prince and his wife the Crown Princess attended the bridge's opening ceremonies in April 1998. Today, at night, the gray-green bridge is set off by 1737 red, green, and blue lights hung along its cables. On holidays or special occasions, the bridge of lights can shimmer in 28 different patterns.

17

Concrete Bridges
(Tavanasa, Salginatobel, Veurdre, Bergsøysund)

An early concrete bridge, Pont Béton

Lime is a mineral with a lot of calcium in it. It usually comes from crushed limestone or chalk. Both are sedimentary rocks made up of piled deposits of shells, coral and skeletons of tiny animals. The tiny sea animals you see here are foramnifera.

Concrete is old. In the 3rd century B.C.E., the Romans began mixing lime with powdered volcanic stone to make a strong, waterproof cement. The Romans added stone rubble to this material and layered it into desired shapes. But when the Empire fell, the knowledge of how to mix concrete appears to have disappeared until late in the 17th century.

Concrete, which people thought of as artificial stone, began to appear in arch bridges around the middle of the 19th century. Like stone, concrete had great compressive strength: it could withstand a lot of weight. But it lacked tensile strength. When subjected to pulling forces, as along the bottom of a beam, it could crack apart.

To add to concrete's tensile strength, people began to lay lengths of iron or steel within it before it set. In 1867, a French gardener named Joseph Monier patented a way of making plant tubs out of cement poured around steel netting. Soon he began building bridges using the same principle. Engineers in the U.S. and Austria experimented with designs of their own. The iron or steel bars resisted stretching. Engineers placed most of them toward the bottom of an arch or beam, where the stretching forces were greatest.

Robert Maillart

Bridges built of this kind of reinforced concrete were fire-resistant and relatively easy to maintain. By 1900, French engineer François Hennebique had designed about a hundred concrete bridges. Instead of imitating thick stone arches, Hennebique began to experiment with lighter, more slender designs. One of Hennebique's assistants expanded this development into an art form. He was the Swiss engineer Robert Maillart.

At first, Maillart anchored his slender concrete arch bridges with old, blocky, solid stone abutments. An example is the Tavanasa Bridge over the Rhine, completed in 1928. Here is the plan for the bridge. Notice the open spandrels, the massive abutments, and the way the supporting structure of the arch is slimmest at the center.

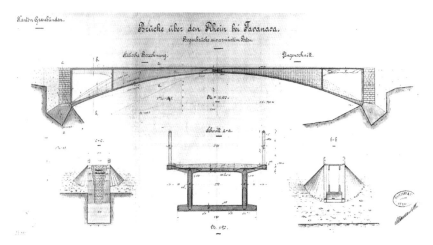

Over time, Maillart's confidence increased. His light and soaring structures crossed rivers and gorges. Perhaps the most beautiful and most famous is his Salginatobel Bridge, built in 1929-1930 in the foothills of the Alps. To build it, a carpenter named Richard Coray first had to construct a framework of timbers that peaked 76 meters (250 feet) above the valley floor. Ninety meters long (295 feet), the bridge has an airy feel. There is no visible abutment where the bridge fits against the canyon wall.

Salginatobel Bridge

Freysinnet: Veurdre Bridge, 1910 and pre-stressed concrete.

A second great builder of concrete bridges was Eugène Freysinnet, who trained at the École des Ponts et Chausées in Paris. "I was born a builder," he liked to say. Growing up in the countryside, he befriended and worked alongside every kind of craftsman: carpenters, blacksmiths, weavers, cabinet makers.

In 1911, as a young graduate, Freysinnet boldly offered to replace three aging bridges across the Allier River for the price another engineering firm wanted to charge for only one. Freysinnet proposed to use concrete instead of stone.

Freysinnet's design called for three concrete segmental arches for each bridge. The roadway would be laid across the top. He started with the Veurdre Bridge. First, he built a supporting timber arch, with each end anchored in its own floating concrete caisson. He fastened the two caissons together so the timber arch would remain stable. Workmen floated the caissons into place and built a concrete arch over the timber arch, three times for the three arches. To allow for the timber support arch to be removed, Freysinnet jacked the two ends of the concrete arch apart, lifting them slightly. Once the timber arch was removed, he let the concrete arms lean down to fit together again.

To Freysinnet's dismay, the concrete began to shrink and deform soon after the arches were complete. It looked as if the concrete, which was so good at resisting pressure (compression), was going to collapse as it gradually pulled apart (tension). Freysinnet gathered up four men and jacked the two sides of each arch apart once more. The men poured more concrete into the gap. The concrete dried and the bridge no longer sagged. It stood until it was destroyed in World War II.

Old Pont du Veurdre

Freysinnet's Pont du Veurdre with later suspension bridge behind.

After that, Freysinnet tested prototypes for each of his bridges. He bound the ends of his concrete arches together with steel rods. Then he measured how the rods came under tension when a load was added to the bridge. He discovered that the concrete continued to shrink for up to a year after it had supposedly dried completely. Freysinnet worked this shrinkage into his plans. Using the method he had invented on the fly for the Veurdre bridge, he left a space at the top of each arch so that he could jack the arch edges slightly apart, tilting the cut ends upward. He filled the gap with more concrete, raising the arches' height by a small amount.

In 1928, Freysinnet filed a patent for the process of pre-stressing concrete, explained below. This process allowed him to strengthen his structures even while using less steel, which reduced both weight and cost.

Bergsøysund, Norway, 1992

Concrete can be used in many different approaches to bridge design, not just in beam or arch bridges. One striking example of a different plan is Norway's Bergsøysund Bridge. Built between two islands along Norway's west coast, the bridge is carried on seven floating concrete pontoons. Construction was completed in 1992 at a price much lower than that of the proposed alternative, a suspension bridge.

Tides float the pontoons up and down by a distance of 4 meters (13 feet), and the bridge is designed to withstand winds of up to 135 kph (84 mph). Each pontoon is anchored in place, but no stays or mooring lines connect one pontoon to any other. The bridge deck running atop the pontoons is framed in steel. Instead of resting just above the water like most pontoon bridges, the Bergsøysund roadway reaches as high as 6 meters (20 feet) above the sea. This elevation means that wa-

Bergsøysund Bridge

ter and sea life can easily pass beneath it, while the road itself is protected from high waves during storms.

More about concrete

Concrete is strong in compression—hard to squash—but only about ten to fifteen percent as strong in tension. This means that an unreinforced concrete beam can fail along the bottom. Concrete is also brittle, so once a crack starts, a beam can break all the way through. The solution to this problem comes in three ways: reinforcing, pre-stressing, and post-tensioning.

The first solution is to reinforce the concrete by placing steel bars across the bottom of the beam as it is poured. The reinforcing bars, called rebar, usually have ridges along their length. These ridges help the concrete and steel cling together.

Steel is strong in tension. It may bend a bit, but it won't break. Reinforced concrete still cracks under tension, but the steel holds it together. The crack doesn't lead to a total break. Sometimes, however, water seeps in through the crack. Water can then rust or corrode the steel, weakening it. Builders sometimes coat the steel bars with waterproof coating, but that can rub off, so engineers monitor the thickness of the steel on older structures to make sure they remain safe.

Rebar

To give concrete even more strength under tension, it can be pre-stressed. Before concrete is poured over the steel bars, the bars are stretched to their greatest length. As the concrete cures or fully dries over the next month, the tension is released on the steel bars, and they tend to shorten slightly, helping to hold the concrete together.

Another approach is called post-tensioning. After concrete is poured, but before it is subjected to any load, workers bore tunnels into it. Through the tunnels, they pass steel cables, called tendons, that are encased in plastic sleeves. The workers anchor each tendon at one end of the tunnel and then jack the other end to around 80 percent of the tension the cable can withstand. Later, when a load is placed on the concrete, the tendon counteracts any tendency for the concrete to deform or pull apart under tension.

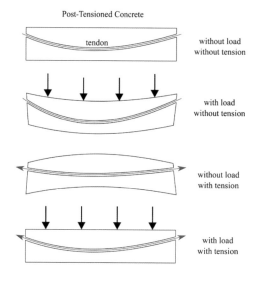

Post-Tensioned Concrete

tendon — without load without tension

with load without tension

without load with tension

with load with tension

These approaches to strengthening concrete allow engineers to build longer, lighter spans. The number of concrete bridges (and buildings) increases every year. Most highway overpasses and new bridges you see every day are probably built of pre-stressed concrete.

About ten billion tons of concrete are manufactured worldwide every year. One downside is that manufacturing concrete releases carbon into the air. In fact, cement manufacture is responsible for as much as seven percent of all the global warming CO_2 we release into the atmosphere each year. Builders can reduce this carbon pollution by adding other materials to concrete. Today, these added materials are often recycled materials such as coal ash, slag, or silica fume, all of which are waste products from other industries. Fly ash, for example, is coal ash that floats out the flue when coal is burned. Nowadays, coal plants are required to capture as much of this polluting ash as possible through filters and electrostatic precipitators. A little less than half of fly ash is recycled, but using it in concrete reduces carbon emissions both at the coal plant and at the concrete plant.

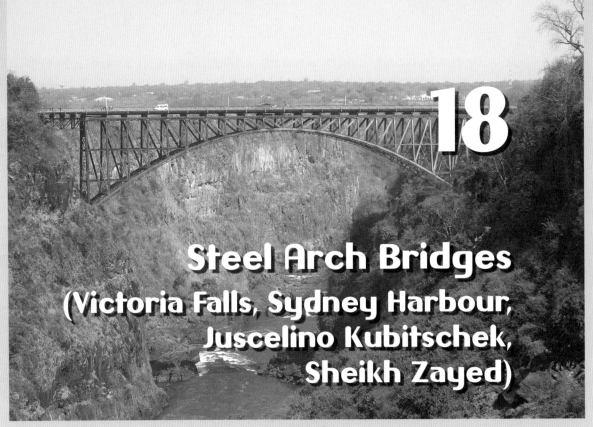

Victoria Falls Bridge

Steel Arch Bridges
(Victoria Falls, Sydney Harbour, Juscelino Kubitschek, Sheikh Zayed)

18

Victoria Falls Bridge, Zambia-Zimbabwe, 1905

CECIL RHODES, A DIAMOND MERCHANT AND POLITICIAN who believed in the glory of the British Empire, dreamt of building a huge railway line across Africa. Running from Egypt south to the Cape of Good Hope, the railway would tie all England's African colonies together. On its way, the railway would cross the great Zambezi River.

On the Zambezi, between the countries of Zambia and Zimbabwe, lie the Victoria Falls, the largest waterfall in the world. Cecil Rhodes never visited the spot, but he insisted that the railways engineers should "build the bridge across the Zambezi where the trains, as they pass, will catch the spray of the Falls."

The consulting designers chose steel and the most traditional of bridge forms, an arch, for their bridge. They had the bridge parts fabricated in London and then shipped them to Mozambique. From there, the bridge parts travelled by rail to the Falls. Although Cecil Rhodes was no longer living by the time construction began in 1904, he would have been impressed by the builders' efficiency. The bridge, 198 meters (650 ft) long, took only 14 months to build.

For fifty years, passenger and cargo trains have crossed the bridge. Trains carried copper, timber, and coal. In 2019, the bridge is still the only rail link between Zambia and Zimbabwe, although sometimes trains pass only at walking pace. The crossing is also one of only three road passageways between the two countries.

The Victoria Falls Bridge is one of southern Africa's top tourist attractions. It even offers a bungee-jumping adventure. With a long, elastic bungee cord strapped to their ankles, adventurers can swan-dive off the parapet.

Author's daughter bungee-jumping off the Victoria Falls Bridge

In 2011, a young Australian woman named Erin Longworthy made the jump. As she reached the bottom of the cord's stretch, it snapped, and she fell the last 24 meters (79 ft) into the water. Luckily, she was a strong swimmer. With her ankles tied together and the broken rope still trailing behind her, she managed to swim among crocodiles, rapids, and whirlpools to the river bank, where she was pulled to safety. Bruised all over and coughing up blood, Longworthy survived. However, getting her to the hospital took hours, because she had come up on the wrong side of the river, in the wrong country, and she wasn't carrying her passport!

Sydney Harbor Bridge, Sydney, Australia, 1932

The world's tallest steel arch bridge crosses Sydney Harbour in New South Wales, Australia. The Sydney Harbour Bridge is a through arch bridge. This means that the base of the arch structure reaches below the bridge deck, but the top of the arch reaches above it. People crossing the bridge travel right through the arch.

Sydney Harbor Bridge, "The Coathanger"

Engineer John Bradfield is considered the father of the bridge. He traveled overseas to examine designs, and decided on a single arch modeled after the Hell Gate Bridge in New York City. The arch design, Bradfield determined, would be cheaper than a beam cantilever bridge.

Builders of steel arch bridges eventually came up with a new idea. The bridge deck doesn't have to go on top of the arch. Instead, it can pass right through!

Construction began in 1923. To start, workers tore down 469 buildings on the northern shore of the harbor. Two hundred fifty Italian, Australian, and Scottish stonemasons quarried granite for use in the two abutment towers.

Work on the arch itself began in 1928. Most of the steel was imported from England, but six million rivets were made in Australia. Each rivet was heated red hot and driven in by hand.

As each side of the arch was built outward from the shore, creeper cranes moved along it. To support the structure, workers dug a tunnel on each end. From an anchor within the tunnel, steel cables ran to the highest part of each half-arch, where they were fastened. This was cantilever construction for an arch bridge. Only when the two halves met in 1930 were the supporting cables released.

Riveting steel plates together was best practice at the time. Today, workers usually join steel parts by welding—melting them together in high heat.

The finished bridge opened in 1932. The top of its arch reaches 134 meters (440 ft) above the water—and up to seven inches higher on hot days due to the steel expanding. Four rail tracks and six lanes of traffic run side by side, allowing trains, cars, trucks, buses, bicycles and pedestrians all to cross at once.

Because it employed so many people during the Great Depression, offering them sustenance and hope, people sometimes called the bridge the Iron Lung. Today, because of its shape, fond citizens call it the Coathanger.

Juscelino Kubitschek Bridge, Brasilia, Brazil, 2002.

In 1955, Juscelino Kubitschek was elected president of Brazil. At once, he began to carry out one of his campaign promises: to build a new capital city. For almost 200 years, Brazil's capital had been the city of Rio de Janeiro, on the southern coast; but the country's constitution called for a

new capital nearer the country's geographic center. So Kubitschek created a design competition for the new capital, to be called Brasilia. City planner Lúcio Costa's plan won the competition, and building began. Brasilia was officially named the country's capital on April 21, 1960. Today it has a population of 2.5 million people.

By the year 2000, it was clear that the two existing bridges across Brasilia's Lake Paranoá were no longer enough to carry the city's traffic. City officials decided on a new bridge, to be named after President Kubitschek. Designer Alexandre Chan and structural engineer Mario Vila Verde won the contract.

The bridge has an unusual, asymmetric design. Three steel arches set diagonally crisscross a roadway. Cables descending from the arches slant down to support the bridge deck. The cables themselves alternate between sides of the bridge in a kind of twisting plane. Altogether, the bridge conveys a feeling of slightly unbalanced movement or even flight. It has been compared to the path of a stone some giant child has set skipping across the water.

The bridge includes five piers, three built in the river and two on the ends. Piles were driven deep into the riverbed's soft mud. Most of the steel components were manufactured on site. First, a steel truss framework was built to support each arch. Then boatmen ferried pieces of the actual bridge out from the shore, and cranes lifted them into place. Workers welded the steel components together. The key components at the arches' tops were welded in at night, when air temperature was stable.

Finally, workers built a steel and concrete bridge deck, held up by cables stretched from the arches. To help with bridge maintenance, workers fitted more than fifty sensors to various locations along the arches and cables.

The Juscelino Kubitshek Bridge opened in 2002. It is 1200 meters long (3900 feet) and 24 meters wide (79 feet). Each span measures 240 meters (790 ft). The bridge's six vehicle lanes are flanked by two lanes reserved for pedestrians.

The bridge harmonizes well with the modern, planned city of Brasilia. In 2003, the year after its completion, designer Alexandre Chan was awarded the 2003 Gustav Lindenthal Medal "for a single, recent outstanding achievement showing harmony with the environment, aesthetic merit and successful community participation."

Sheikh Zayed Bridge, Abu Dhabi, 2010

Abu Dhabi is the world's richest city. Its oil reserves have helped make its 420,000 citizens worth about $17 million each. So naturally, when the island city decided to build a third bridge to connect it to the mainland, the city's government wanted something spectacular. They turned to the world's top woman architect, the Iraqi-born Zaha Hadid. Hadid was famous

Zaha Hadid

for her unique, curved structures, which she designed using computerized programs she created herself.

Hadid came up with a truly original design. Her three steel arches run in a single continuous wave from one side of the Makhta channel to the other. The arches rise in parallel with the roadway, then swoop down to the water and rise again. The undulating design echoes the contours of desert sand dunes.

The steel arches are anchored in piers built of reinforced concrete. Blocks of concrete also connect the parallel arches together. Cables extend down from the arches to support the concrete bridge deck. The roadway is divided, with four travel lanes and one emergency lane running each way. At one end of the bridge, the double roadway runs between the parallel arches. At the other end, the roadway rests on cantilevers extending to the arches' sides.

The bridge is 842 meters (2,760 ft) long and 64 meters (210 ft) high. The gently rising roadway crests at 20 meters (66 feet) above water level.

Abu Dhabi named the bridge for the founder of the United Arab Emirates, Sheikh Zayed bin Sultan Al Nahyan. Construction took seven years, about twice as long as originally planned. Sheikh Zayed's son Sheikh Khalifa opened the bridge on November 25, 2010.

One of the bridge's most striking features is its lighting, designed by Dutch lighting engineer Rogier van der Heide. Van der Heide programmed more than 200 colored lights to play in 13 different lighting patterns to celebrate different occasions.

19

Cable-Stayed Bridges

Alamillo Bridge

I N A SUSPENSION BRIDGE, WIRES HANG DOWN FROM THE overhead suspension cables strung between high towers. The vertical hanging wires support the bridge deck. In a cable-stayed bridge, there are no suspension cables. Instead, the cables that support the bridge run directly from pylons (towers) to the roadway. These stiff cables are called stays, and they can be arranged in different ways to make the bridge both strong and beautiful.

Basic design of a cable-stayed bridge

Probably the first person to design a cable-stayed bridge was a Venetian inventor during the Renaissance named Fausto Veranzio. In 1595, in his book *Machinae Novae* (New Devices), Veranzio included a drawing of a bridge deck held up by ropes fanning out from stone towers on either side of a river.

Many early suspension bridges, like the Brooklyn Bridge, added stays to make the bridges stiffer and more stable.

In the past thirty years, cable-stayed bridge design has spread across the world. Different countries have come up with striking variations. One early proponent of cable-stayed design is the Spanish architect, sculptor and engineer Santiago Calavara.

Alamillo Bridge, Seville, 1992

In 1992, Spain held the World's Fair, Expo '92, on a deserted island in the Guadalquivir River in Seville. The city decided to build two bridges to the island in preparation for the fair. The Alamillo Bridge, spanning 200 meters across the river, is suspended from a single pylon. This pylon, 142 meters high (466 feet), leans back from the bridge at an angle of 58 degrees above the horizontal. The weight of the leaning pylon helps acts as a counterweight to the load held up by thirteen pairs of cables.

Alamillo Bridge from the roadway

To build the pylons, a large crane lifted hollow steel segments into place. Workers welded them together and filled them with reinforced concrete. The roadway itself is built of steel box girders. Just above road level, steel wings cantilevered off the main spine of the bridge allow pedestrians and bicycles to cross safely.

Samuel Beckett Bridge, Dublin, 2009

Calavara designed another beautiful bridge seventeen years later, this time in Dublin, Ireland. The Samuel Beckett Bridge, named after Ireland's great playwright and novelist, crosses the River Liffey. It uses 31 cable stays. Once again Calavara chose a single leaning pylon. This time the pylon leans into the bridge instead of leaning back. Two massive cables anchor the pylon to the shore behind. The leaning pylon and parallel strings are designed to resemble a harp, the national symbol of Ireland.

Samuel Beckett Bridge

Calavara claims that the inspiration for the design came to him when he was spinning an Irish coin, which has a Celtic harp on the back. To make the spinning coin comparison stronger, the Samuel Beckett Bridge is actually movable. When ships need to pass up or downriver, the entire harp section rotates clockwise ninety degrees from the base of the pylon to lie against the shore. Opening or closing takes about two minutes.

Millau Viaduct, Tarn Valley, 2004

The Millau Viaduct's towers are taller than the Eiffel Tower. (And it's pronounced "Mee-YO.")

The world's tallest bridge is a cable-stayed bridge over a gorge in the valley of the Tarn River in southern France. The French government decided in the 1990s that a long, high bridge between two limestone plateaus was needed to relieve the traffic that choked the bottom of the valley. So began a long period of planning and design competitions for various engineering firms.

In 1996, a judging committee selected a cable-stayed design by the English architect Lord Norman Foster and the French structural engineer Michel Virlogeux. Still, it took until 2001 before all the details were worked out and a construction company was selected. The Eiffage company agreed to build the bridge at its own expense in return for the right to collect tolls (currently about 8 to 10 Euros) for the next 75 years.

Building the bridge took only three years. First, the construction firm dug four 15-meter (50-ft) deep shafts for each of the bridge's seven pylons. Three months later, the pylons started to rise above the ground at a rate of more than a meter per day. Hydraulic jacks worked their way up the structure, adding supports as they climbed. A new layer of concrete could be poured every twenty minutes. Eight temporary towers were also raised to help support the bridge during construction.

Meanwhile, the steel roadway was being prepared on the land ends of the viaduct. Once ready, it was rolled out between the pylons, under computer control. Finally, workers trucked pieces of the masts (top parts of the pylons) to their proper places along the road. Lying on the roadway, the pieces were welded together and then tilted into place. Finally, eleven stays, arranged in a harp design, were installed to connect each mast to the bridge deck. At this point, workers removed the temporary towers, and the bridge stood on its own.

The health of this bridge is being constantly monitored as if it were a patient in intensive care!

Engineers included a range of the most up-to-date safety monitoring equipment in the bridge. They built in sensors of all kinds. The simplest are temperature gauges. Accelerometers like those in your cell phone measure movement under the weight of traffic on the bridge deck. Extensometers at the base of the tallest pylons can measure any change in length that comes from stress and strain, tension and compression. The extensometers measure changes as small as one micrometer, which is one-thousandth of a millimeter. Piezoelectric sensors, which convert changes in pressure to electrical signals, monitor the passage of traffic.

As for the cables, they too are designed for maximum safety. Each stay is made of 55 to 91 steel strands. Each strand has three coatings to resist corrosion: they are galvanized with tin, coated in petroleum wax, and covered in a polyethylene sheath.

Millau Viaduct

The finished bridge opened on December 16, 2004, almost a month ahead of schedule. Construction cost close to 400 million euros, which at the time was more than 500 million dollars. The bridge is 2,460 meters (8,070 ft) long, and the top of the tallest pier rises 343 meters (1,125 ft) above its base. In 2006, the Millau Viaduct received the Outstanding Structure award from the International Association for Bridge and Structural Engineering. The award announcement cited it not only for its beauty as "an elegant, slender bridge soaring above a deep valley" but also for the innovative manner in which it was built.

The last two cable-stayed bridges I want to mention are both in the United States. Both use a method called the cradle system for their stays.

Leonard B. Zakim Bunker Hill Memorial Bridge, Boston, 2002

Local people call it the Bunker Hill Bridge; most others call it the Zakim Bridge. Completed in 2003, it forms part of Boston's Big Dig, which is the largest highway construction project the U.S. has ever taken on. The Big Dig raised a highway, built a tunnel under Boston Harbor, and eased traffic flow through the city's congested center. It also built a hybrid steel and concrete bridge across the Charles River.

The bridge is named after a Boston civil rights activist named Leonard Zakim who promoted "bridges between people." At the same time, the bridge towers were designed to echo the look of the nearby monument honoring colonial militiamen who fell at the Battle of Bunker Hill.

The bridge has two towers shaped like upside-down Ys. Instead of attaching directly to the towers, cables run from one part of the bridge deck

Zakim Bridge

through a "cradle" or tunnel in the tower to a part of the deck beyond the tower. That way, two sections of the deck help to balance each other.

The Zakim Bridge is one of the widest cable-stayed bridges in the world. Although only 436 meters (1,432 ft) long, it is 56 meters (183 ft) wide. Four lanes of traffic travel in each direction. Two more northbound lanes travel on a cantilever outside the stays.

To allow for the bridge abutments, the contours of the Charles River had to be rearranged. This re-shaping of the shoreline required environmental permits and careful planning. Under the bridge, the city installed landscaping and public art structures. Five perforated stainless steel sculptures are lit up at night in a piece called "Five Beacons for the Lost Half-Mile."

The bridge had a "soft opening" on Mother's Day in May 2002. On that rainy Sunday, 200,000 people waited for their turns to cross the bridge. On October 4, 2002, Bruce Springsteen sang "Thunder Road" at the bridge's official dedication. Ten days after that, 14 circus elephants marched across the Zakim Bridge, "testing" it with their combined weight of 51,000 kilograms (112,000 pounds). This event was a historical reference to the elephants that tested the Eads Bridge and Brooklyn Bridge.

The Zakim Bridge didn't actually open to traffic until early 2003, when the roadway connecting it to the Central Artery Tunnel through the city was finally completed.

Penobscot Narrows Bridge, Bangor, Maine, 2006

The Penobscot Narrows Bridge crosses the Penobscot River below Bangor along the Maine coast. It replaced a 70-year-old suspension bridge that was showing signs of wear in its cables and deck. Planning and building the new bridge took less than four years.

The Penobscot Narrows Bridge is 646 meters (2,120 feet) long and only two lanes wide. Its cables consist of multiple steel strands. Sheathed within a 2.5-centimeter (1 inch) steel tube, each strand passes through a cradle opening in one of the bridge towers. The cables tie the bridge together and suspend it from the towers. This design means that each strand can be examined, removed or replaced separately. Six strands have been replaced with carbon fibers to test this new material. Someday, carbon fibers may take over from steel in bridge construction.

One of the bridge's two towers contains the Penobscot Bridge Observatory, one of only four bridge observatories in the world. At 420 feet (130 m) high, the observatory is the tallest occupied structure in Maine. Luckily, it's also served by one of Maine's fastest elevators. Through the observatory windows, visitors can admire a 360-degree view, including the bridge, Penobscot Bay and the nearby Fort Knox.

In December of 2013, large chunks of ice began to fall from the cables onto the road deck. Two cars were destroyed and several others damaged. Bridge authorities closed the bridge for one day and again a week later as they waited for the ice to melt and fall.

Similar problems have occurred on other cable-stayed bridges in cold climates, and people have tried a number of solutions. In some places, engineers have tried heating the stays directly or by blowing hot air on them; elsewhere they have treated the stays with a chemical solution. British Columbia chose a mechanical solution. Mechanisms called cable sweepers are fitted around the cable and then sent riding up and down the cable to reduce ice buildup. But for now, the most practical approach seems to be to monitor temperature and humidity, predict when the problem might occur, and send traffic on a 40-mile detour when there's a risk of falling ice.

Penobscot Narrows Bridge

20

Longest Bridges
(Lake Pontchartrain, Hangzhou Bay, Danyang Kunshan, HKZM)

Hong Kong-Zhuhai-Macau Bridge

Lake Pontchartrain Causeway Bridge

A CAUSEWAY IS USUALLY A TRACK ACROSS a "low or wet place." In southeastern Louisiana, that wet place is a lake, and the causeway is a low-lying bridge.

Lake Pontchartrain is an estuary, which means it's the mouth of a large river. In fact, the entire area used to be part of the outflow of the Mississippi River. But around 4000 years ago, the meandering river started depositing enough silt that it eventually walled off the lake and flowed to the south of it. Choctaws called the lake Okwa-ta, which means "wide water." In 1699, a French explorer renamed it after the French minister of marine affairs, Count Pontchartrain. Eighteen years later,

French settlers founded New Orleans just south of the lake, which allowed easy navigation from the ocean all the way through the lake to the city.

Five smaller rivers still flow into Lake Pontchartrain, and a narrow strait still connects it to the Gulf of Mexico. The lake is wide and shallow, with an average depth of only about 13 feet (4 meters) but a total area of 630 square miles (1600 square kilometers). Its brackish waters, where salt water from the ocean mixes with fresh river water, rise and fall slightly with the tide. All around the lake is a huge wetland in an area of swamp cypress, hardwood forests, and underwater plants. From clams and freshwater mussels to paddlefish and sturgeon, to manatees and sharks,

Lake Pontchartrain from southbound causeway

to woodpeckers, brown pelicans and migrating seabirds, the lake's ecosystem forms a rich web.

Today, a bridge crosses Lake Pontchartrain—the longest continuous bridge over water found anywhere in the world. At its longest point, it is 23.8 miles (38.4 km). But like many of the bridges we've encountered in these pages, the Lake Pontchartrain Causeway lingered in the planning stage for decades. A man named Bernard de Marigny, who founded the town of Mandeville across the lake from New Orleans, first proposed the idea in the early 1800s. When no one took him up on it, he opened a ferry service instead. In the 1920s, someone proposed building a bridge across a set of artificial islands that could be used for expensive homes. No one backed that idea either. But finally, in 1948, the Louisiana legislature created the Causeway Commission to come up with a plan.

A two-lane bridge opened in 1956. A toll bridge, it connected Mandeville on the north side of the lake to the New Orleans suburb of Metaire on the south side. Thirteen years later, a parallel roadway opened two more lanes of traffic right alongside. The long, low, four-lane bridge is built of beams laid atop 9,500 concrete pilings. Eight miles from the north shore, a bascule opens for passing ships.

On August 29, 2005, the ferociously destructive Hurricane Katrina came ashore just east of New Orleans. A storm surge drove Lake Pontchartrain to burst through protective barriers and cascade into the city. Amazingly, the raging winds and water destroyed only 17 spans of the Causeway. Within a couple of weeks, emergency vehicles were crossing the bridge again, and on September 19, the bridge opened to general traffic.

For one month, people even got to cross the bridge toll-free.

Hangzhou Bay Bridge, Zhejiang, China, 2008

When it opened in 2008, the 36-kilometer (22-mile) bridge across Hangzhou Bay was the longest bridge over ocean water in the world. The bridge, which crosses between the cities of Jiaxing and Ningbo along China's east coast, took nine years to plan and four to build.

The Lake Pontchartrain Bridge is longer, but it crossed an estuary, not part of an ocean.

Engineers planning the bridge faced serious obstacles. Hangzhou Bay and the mouth of the Qiantang River (already mentioned in Chapter 10) boast of one of the strongest tidal surges in the world. The tide runs at two to three km/sec, and waves can reach a height of 8 meters (26 ft). During typhoon season, winds may howl across the bay at speeds greater than 150 kilometers per hour (93 mph). Added to that, deep mud flats on the eastern end of the bridge made for a difficult construction problem. No wonder the builders asked for 120 technical studies before they completed their plans.

The engineers designed a concrete box girder bridge set on steel pilings. The bridge makes a shallow S as it crosses the bay, allowing the tides to pass while applying the least possible force. The center two spans of the bridge, each 443 meters long and 62 meters high, allow modern container

Hangzhou Bay Bridge

vessels to pass beneath. To support these longer spans, cable stays fan out from two triangular towers.

As construction began, engineers identified a new problem: fifteen meters below the seabed lay a lake of methane, or natural gas. To avoid issues of collapsing ground or a possible methane explosion, workers carefully drove pipes into the pool to vent the methane. Only six months later, with the methane long gone, did they begin driving piles into the sea floor.

Workers constructed the steel pilings on shore and then carried them into place on special ships. The ship pilots relied on GPS to direct them to the precise spot for each piling. From a steel framework aboard ship, hydraulic hammers drove the piles—5600 of them— deep into the seabed.

All the pilings ended up within 5 centimeters (2 inches) of where they were supposed to be!

Back on shore, the crew constructed sections of concrete box girder, each weighing 2000 tons. To carry them out to the cranes across the strip of soft sand along the shore, workers used a huge truck with 640 wheels. Once the girder sections reached the water, giant floating cranes hoisted them and carried them to the right spot. Eight anchors held each crane in place as it lifted and positioned the girders.

In June 2007, construction workers triumphantly joined the two ends of the bridge together. Two weeks later, officials held an opening ceremony. Eleven months of testing followed. Finally, in May 2008, the Hangzhou Bay Bridge opened to the public. Three lanes of highway carried traffic in each direction.

In 2010, a new, 10,000 square meter (100,000 sq ft) service center opened on a platform constructed next to the center of the bridge. Called Land Between Sea and Sky, it holds restaurants, a shopping mall, space for exhibitions, and an observation tower. About 50,000 vehicles a year cross the bridge, which shortens their trip between Shanghai and Ningbo by two hours. Officials expect that tolls from the crossing will pay off the $1.7

Hangzhou Bay Bridge

billion cost of the bridge in twelve to fifteen years.

Danyang-Kunshan Grand Bridge, Shanghai to Nanjing, China, 2011

Chinese engineers keep designing longer and longer bridges. The current record holder crosses land as one extremely long raised railway bed. The Danyang-Kunshan viaduct carries high-speed trains 165 km (102 mi) from Shanghai to Nanjing.

The viaduct crosses the delta of the Yangtze, one of China's two great rivers. It traverses canals, marshes, lakes, rivers, and rice paddies. One 9-km section crosses a lake in the ancient canal city of Suzhou.

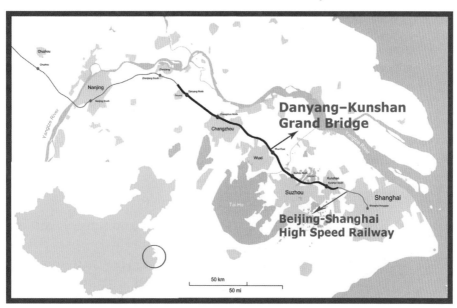

Thick red line shows the track of the railway bridge

Ten thousand people worked four years, at a cost of $8.5 billion, to construct the viaduct, which consists of concrete girders between concrete piers. Trains on the viaduct reach speeds between 250 and 300 kph (155-186 mph). The viaduct is the southern end of the Beijing to Shanghai line, which is China's most profitable rail line, carrying 180 million passengers a year.

These speeds seem incredible without maglev. They show how smooth the bridge must be.

At first the railway authorities considered using maglev technology on the bridge—short for magnetic levitation. A maglev train doesn't need an engine. Instead, the walls and track carry strong electric coils that create a powerful magnetic field. This field repels large magnets attached to the underside of the train. The train levitates slightly, riding on a cushion of air above the track. The decrease in friction allows the train to travel very fast. But in the end, the railway from Shanghai to Nanjing stuck with steel wheels on steel tracks.

Section of Danyang-Kunshang Bridge

Hong Kong-Zhuhai-Macau Bridge, Pearl River Delta, 2018

The *Guinness Book of World Records* currently lists a new Chinese bridge as its record holder for the longest (discontinuous) bridge over water. The structure is a three-part bridge over the Pearl River Estuary, the body of water which separates the island of Hong Kong from the Chinese mainland. Xi Jinping, president of the People's Republic of China, opened the Hong Kong-Macau-Zhuhai Bridge on October 24, 2018. Water once negotiated only by ferries can now be crossed by cars, buses and trucks. Overall, the HKZM bridge is 34.2 mi (55 km) long.

Remember, the Pontchartrain Causeway is the longest **continuous** bridge over water. Little tweaks in definitions allow more bridges into the record book!

The idea of a combined bridge and tunnel crossing the Pearl River Estuary was first raised thirty years earlier, by a businessman named Gordon Wu. He was inspired by the Chesapeake Bay Bridge and Tunnel, a 37 km (23 mi) crossing on the coast of Virginia. At the time, the British still ruled Hong Kong, and they were not thrilled with the idea. Even after the British transferred control of Hong Kong to China in 1997, coordinating efforts among the three large cities of Hong Kong, Zhuhai, and Macau was not easy.

Work on the bridge finally began on the mainland side in late 2009. On the Hong Kong side, an environmental lawsuit delayed the start until two years later. Citizens and organizations, including the World Wildlife Fund, worried about the effect of the bridge on the small surviving population of Pearl River dolphins. These light-colored, pinkish-white dolphins are a subspecies of a variety of dolphin found only in southeastern Asia. Conservation groups convinced the Chinese government to create protected parks

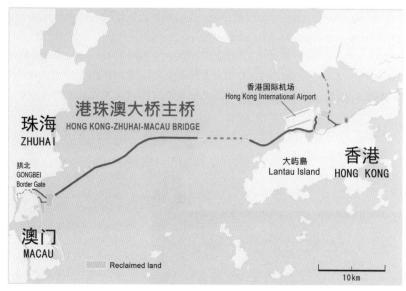

Dotted line shows the tunnel section of the bridge

within the Pearl River Estuary to make sure the remaining dolphins would have a safe home and plenty of fish to eat.

Building the bridge was a huge undertaking. Most of the bridge is a beam or trestle design, with a fairly low profile and many piers. At two sections along the main, central part of the bridge, the bridge deck is cable-stayed. To allow ship traffic to pass, the builders laid down two artificial islands almost 6.7 km (4.3 mi) apart in the waters to the west of Hong Kong. Between these two islands, they constructed the world's longest undersea tunnel. The tunnel carries three lanes of traffic in each direction, while overhead, ships pass without pause.

Not everything went smoothly during construction. In the past, deaths among bridge workers were so common they were accepted as part of the price of bridge-building. Today's public, in contrast, demands accountability for such tragedies. Nineteen people died while building the HKZM bridge. In 2107, an independent Hong Kong commission arrested 21 bridge employees for falsifying test results about concrete quality. Three technicians went to jail for corruption.

Hong Kong, Macau, and the mainland government of China shared the cost of building the bridge, which was about 127 billion yuan, equal to almost $19 billion. Tolls on the bridge are expected to raise $86 million a year, meaning that it will take more than 200 years for tolls to return the investment. Still, authorities claim that the bridge will help pay for itself through increased trade generated by reducing travel time among the three cities.

And what about the dolphins? Their numbers did drop while the bridge was being built. Researchers blamed the drop on high speed ferries and habitat loss, as part of the river was lost to the artificial islands. Researchers are watching carefully to see if the population can recover.

21

Six Bridge Disasters
(Ponte das Barcas, Tay Railway Bridge, Quebec, Tacoma Narrows, Tangiwai, Silver Bridge)

CROSSING A BRIDGE IS AN ACT OF TRUST. WE TRUST THAT the bridge will hold, that the structure won't collapse. But every once in a while, bridges give out, often dramatically. They fail because of poor design, shoddy materials, construction errors, or half-hearted maintenance. And even with well-built bridges, disasters can happen: floods, landslides, earthquakes, fire, bitter cold, or tearing winds. The flow of water may undermine bridges. Too many people or vehicles may crowd onto them. Ships, airplanes, trucks or even derailed trains may crash into them. Then gravity does its work!

In this chapter we'll look at a few historic collapses and the reasons behind them. But please remember, bridge disasters are rare!

Overload: Ponte das Barcas, Portugal, 1809

One of the greatest bridge disasters of all time occurred in the Portuguese city of Porto. In 1809, Napoleon's army invaded Portugal, rampaging through the countryside. On March 29, French troops under Marshal Soult defeated the Portuguese troops and moved towards the city. The following day, the panicked population crowded on the banks of the river Douro, frantic to cross the water to escape the advancing army. Their bridge was a pontoon bridge, a "Bridge of Boats," barges bound together by steel cables. Thousands of people, carrying all they could, herding children and animals ahead of them and hauling carts full of goods, swarmed onto the narrow bridge.

A Catástrofe da Ponte das Barcas, the Bridge of Boats Disaster, 1809

They were too many. The boats dipped below water level. Water poured over their thwarts, even as more people pushed onto the bridge on the Porto side. As the barges swamped and sank, each boat dragged down the next by the chains connecting them. With gunfire sounding behind, thousands of people, weighed down by their clothes and possessions, plunged into the water. Four thousand civilians died.

Design flaws and wind, Tay Bridge, Scotland, 1879

A railway bridge over the Firth of Tay, between Dundee and Wormit, Scotland, opened in 1878 after seven years of construction. The bridge engineer, Thomas Bouch, designed the bridge to be supported by iron piers. His plan called for a lattice truss to support a deck with one track along a length of about 3000 meters (10,000 ft). However, once construction began, workers discovered that the bedrock on which the piers would sit lay deeper than they had thought. Accordingly, Bouch altered his design to use fewer piers and longer girders. These changes reduced the overall strength of the bridge.

Tay Bridge before the disaster

For an earlier bridge, Bouch had asked an expert for advice about wind forces. For the Tay Bridge, he didn't bother.

Queen Victoria rode across the bridge on June 20, 1879. She was so pleased, she knighted Bouch six days later. But on the evening of December 28, disaster struck.

In the early darkness, a violent storm began to blow, with winds up to 70 mph (110 kph) blowing at right angles to the bridge. At 7:13 pm, a train started from the southern end across the bridge. An observer witnessed what happened next: For three minutes, sparks rose from the train's wheels. Then, when the train reached the middle of the bridge, a bright light flashed, followed by sudden darkness.

The entire middle section of the bridge had collapsed into the river, with the train trapped among the girders. Seventy-five people drowned. Many of their bodies were never found. An exhaustive court of inquiry turned up several damning pieces of information. Bouch had failed to adjust his design for potential windstorms. In particular, the cross-bracing of the piers was probably not sufficient to withstand high winds. Moreover, work in the foundry had been sloppy, with poor oversight, so the iron in the piers and girders may have been substandard. Finally, the man charged with inspecting the completed bridge actually knew very little about iron.

One of the examiners wrote, "Can there be any doubt that what caused the overthrow of the bridge was the pressure of the wind acting upon a structure badly built and badly maintained?"

Tay bridge disaster, 1879

The disaster ruined the reputation of Sir Thomas Bouch, who died less than a year after the train fell.

Although only 46 bodies were ever recovered from the river, the engine itself was hauled ashore and put back into service for forty more years. Railwaymen dubbed the resurrected engine "The Diver."

The Tay Bridge catastrophe remains Great Britain's worst train disaster. Another small disaster was a poem written to commemorate it. The writer was William McGonagall, who preferred to call himself The Knight of the White Elephant of Burmah. According to a website created in his honor, McGonagall "has been widely hailed as the worst poet in the English language." His sorrowful (and sorry) poem on the disaster concludes,

Oh! ill-fated Bridge of the Silv'ry Tay,
I must now conclude my lay
By telling the world fearlessly without the least dismay,
That your central girders would not have given way,
At least many sensible men do say,
Had they been supported on each side with buttresses,
At least many sensible men confesses,
For the stronger we our houses do build,
The less chance we have of being killed.

William McGonagall

Faulty design: Quebec Bridge, 1907

The Quebec Bridge across the St. Lawrence River, part of Canada's Transcontinental Railway system, was going to be the longest in the world. To oversee the bridge's construction, which began in 1904, the Quebec Bridge Company hired the American bridge engineer, Theodore Cooper, a man with a high regard for himself. Of the bridge plans submitted, Cooper selected a cantilever design. The bridge would stand 150 feet above the water. Anchor arms 500 feet long would project from piers on either shore. A 1600-foot center span would connect the two arms. This was the "best and the cheapest" design, Cooper pronounced. But he made one change, increasing the center span to 1800 feet in length.

Cooper was busy, so didn't oversee construction on site. He preferred to stay in New York City, relying on two local engineers to manage day-to-day issues. But Cooper also didn't like other people interfering. When the Canadian government wanted to hire its own expert to review calculations about how much the steel bridge would weigh, Cooper objected, and the government gave in.

After the Quebec Bridge collapse, 1907

Work went well for the first couple of years. But in June 1907, inspecting engineer Norman McLure wired Cooper about some misalignment of support chords—the lower outside horizontal pieces—in the south anchor arm. Cooper wired back, "Make as good work of it as you can. It is not serious." The team jacked the two parts into alignment, but two months later, McLure telegraphed Cooper again. Some of the bars were bending. Over the course of one week, the end of chord 9-L moved by one and a half inches. McLure visited New York to talk to Cooper.

Worried, Cooper wired to the company to "add no more load to the bridge till after due consideration of the facts." But construction did not stop right away. Late that afternoon, a construction worker named Beauvais noticed that a rivet he had driven earlier that day had snapped in two. Just as he called out to tell his foreman, the bridge collapsed with a shriek of twisting, tearing metal. The southern arm of the cantilever plummeted into the river, taking 86 workers with it. Some, like Beauvais, escaped with only broken limbs, but 74 died, either crushed or drowned.

It turned out that the steel used in the bridge was much heavier than the official plan had prescribed. The bridge was not strong enough to carry its own dead load—the weight of the bridge alone, with nobody on it.

Clearing the mess of tangled steel from the river took two years. The government hired a new engineer and selected a fresh design, with heavier,

Floating center span downstream to rebuild the Quebec Bridge, 1916

When the bridge fell, people 10 miles away felt the earth shake.

stronger cantilever arms. This time the design was better, but the Company's construction methods were far from flawless. In 1916, as a crane was lifting the center span into place, it fell into the river, killing 13 men.

More wind: Tacoma Narrows Bridge, 1940

Suspension bridges were all the rage in the 1930s. Soon after the Golden Gate opened, construction began on another, even lighter and more elegant bridge over the Tacoma Narrows in Washington state. This was the Tacoma Narrows Bridge, which became famous for its spectacular collapse just three months after opening.

Its original design called for a stiffening truss supporting the bridge deck, similar to that used in the Golden Gate. But Leon Moisseiff, the New

Official Opening

TACOMA
NARROWS BRIDGE
AND
McCHORD FIELD

June 30 --- July 4, 1940, A. D.

York engineer who had worked on the Golden Gate, approached authorities with a slimmer, less expensive design. Instead of a 25-foot deep truss arrangement of diagonal supports below the bridge deck, he proposed using plate girders only 8 feet deep. These stiff, solid steel beams, he assured them, would be enough to keep the road deck steady. Authorities selected Moisseiff's design at a savings of $3 million.

Building the bridge took only nineteen months. Only two traffic lanes wide, with a main span 2,800 feet (850 m) long, the bridge had a light and elegant profile. But whenever the wind blew, the bridge deck rose and fell in waves, leading construction workers to nickname the bridge "Galloping Gertie." Engineers made several attempts to stabilize it. For example, they attached cables from the plate girders to concrete blocks on shore. However, when the wind rose, the cables snapped.

Even on opening day, July 1, 1940, members of the public noticed the bridge's movement. As traffic on the bridge increased thereafter, the authorities hired an engineering professor named Frederick Burt Farquharson to suggest a remedy. Farquharson and his students at the University of Washington built a wind tunnel and scale models of the bridge and bridge deck. They proposed two solutions. The first was to drill holes in the girders and deck to allow the wind to pass through. Officials rejected this solution as irreversible and too involved. The second was to give the bridge a more aerodynamic shape by adding deflectors at its sides. The authorities selected this option, but before it could be implemented, and just five days after the study concluded, the wind took over.

Throughout the morning of November 7, 1940, as winds rose to about 40 mph, the undulations of the bridge increased. The bridge began not only to rise and fall, but also to twist. Spectators gathered. An editor of the Tacoma News Tribune named Leonard Coatsworth was the last person to try to drive across the bridge. At one point he got out to examine the roadway. When he started back toward his car, he saw it sliding from side to side on the tilting, undulating deck.

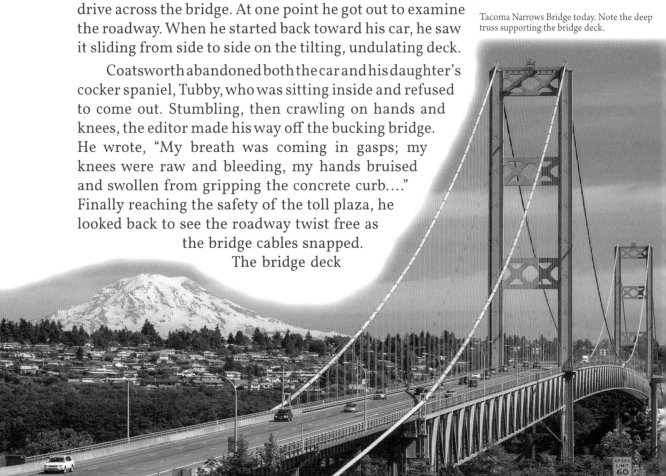

Tacoma Narrows Bridge today. Note the deep truss supporting the bridge deck.

Coatsworth abandoned both the car and his daughter's cocker spaniel, Tubby, who was sitting inside and refused to come out. Stumbling, then crawling on hands and knees, the editor made his way off the bucking bridge. He wrote, "My breath was coming in gasps; my knees were raw and bleeding, my hands bruised and swollen from gripping the concrete curb...." Finally reaching the safety of the toll plaza, he looked back to see the roadway twist free as the bridge cables snapped.

The bridge deck

broke, dangled, and plunged into the waters below.

Analysis of how the bridge failed began at once, aided by film taken of its final minutes. High school physics classes often show this Tacoma Narrows footage as an example of resonance, a mechanical phenomenon in which oscillation, or repeated waves of motion, can increase. This can cause vibration that damages or destroys structures. The truth is more complicated. Modern engineers speak of "aeroelastic fluttering," an extreme type of vibration that can occur in water or air. They note how the two halves of the bridge twisted in opposite directions.

Plans to rebuild the bridge began soon after its failure. This time, every possible design was tested in a wind tunnel. Two issues delayed construction. The first was that World War II meant a shortage of steel: it was all going to build airplanes and ships. The second was that the state of Washington couldn't find an insurance company willing to cover the new bridge.

Construction finally resumed in 1948. The new bridge used a truss support system under the roadway, as engineers had originally proposed. This design proved stable, and traffic gradually increased. A third bridge, parallel to the replacement bridge, opened in 2012 to allow even more cars to cross.

Natural disaster: Tangiwai, New Zealand, 1953

On Christmas Eve of 1953, an express train from Wellington to Auckland on the North Island of New Zealand hurtled through the darkness. The passengers were traveling to visit loved ones for the holiday—second class passengers in the first five cars, where there was the most noise and smoke, and first class passengers in the last four cars.

In the Maori language, "Tangiwai" means "weeping water" or "river of tears."

The train passed through the Tangiwai station at 10:20 pm, moving at 40 mph (60 kph). The next landmark was a bridge over the small Whangaehu River. The bridge was only 300 feet (90 m) long, the weather was good, the engine was running smoothly, and there was nothing to worry the engineer.

Upstream, the Ruapehu volcano lay dormant. It had last erupted eight years earlier, in 1945. The eruption left a crater that gradually filled with water. A natural dam made of rocks and volcanic particles held this lake high in the mountains—for eight years. Now, suddenly, the dam broke, setting loose a **lahar**—a flood of water, mud, ice, and rock. A violent wave 20 feet (6 m) high surged into and down the Whangaehu River.

Just downstream from the railway bridge stood a bridge for motor vehicles. As a man named Cyril Ellis approached it, he saw to his amazement that a flood of water was pouring over the bridge. Realizing at once the danger to the oncoming train, he ran up the bank, waving his flashlight and shouting. Maybe the train driver saw him, because later evidence showed that he applied the brakes 200 yards before the bridge.

Too late. The lahar had crumpled one of the bridge's concrete pylons, causing the train bed to collapse into the river. The locomotive, tender, and first five cars hurtled over the broken track and into the river. The sixth car teetered on the edge.

Ellis grabbed the train guard from the back of the train, and the two of them ran up to the sixth car, shouting to the passengers inside to exit through the back. But before any could respond, the dangling car broke loose from those behind it and fell, dragging Cooper, the guard, and 22 passengers along with it.

Crater Lake at Ruapehu volcano, New Zealand

As the train car lay half submerged, the two men managed to break a window. They boosted 21 passengers outside to the top of the carriage. As the lahar passed, they organized a human chain to pull the passengers to safety on the riverbank. From the sixth car, only one passenger, a young girl, died.

The second-class passengers in the first five cars were not as lucky. Most drowned or died of injuries as their cars were crushed by the torrent. Some,

After the lahar passed, Tangiwai, 1953

swept downstream, managed to make their way out of the river, covered in mud and oil. Rescuers took these survivors to a nearby army field hospital to be treated for cold and shock. Meanwhile, the surge of water receded almost as fast as it had risen. Now the train cars lay strewn along the banks.

Nearby residents, who had heard the roar as the lahar swept through, quickly summoned help. Army units combed the river banks, hauling the bodies back to the field hospital all through Christmas day. Corpses continued to float to the surface for the next month, but twenty passengers were never found. In all, 151 people died, including two engineers and all but 28 of the second-class passengers.

The Queen of England, visiting New Zealand on a state visit, made a special radio broadcast on Christmas Day to mourn the victims. Prince Philip attended a mass funeral a few days after.

An inquiry found no fault with the railway department or any of its personnel. Still, after the accident, the railway installed a lahar warning system upstream. In 2007, the alarm sounded when another lahar burst out. Warned in time, the trains halted. On that occasion, no bridges collapsed and no lives were lost.

The Tangiwai River disaster remains New Zealand's worst rail accident.

Manufacturing defect and poor maintenance: Silver Bridge, Ohio River 1967

A steel suspension bridge over the Ohio River between West Virginia and Ohio, the Silver Bridge was finished in 1928. In place of the multitude of woven steel wires used in many suspension bridges, the Silver Bridge used suspension chains built of **eyebars**.

An eyebar is a length of steel both ends of which have been flattened, then pierced by holes or "eyes." Pins passing through these holes into similar holes in another eyebar attach them together. Eyebar chains were usually built with four to six bars next to each other, like a bundle of sticks.

That way, if one failed, the others would still hold, and the chain itself would not part. The builders of the Silver Bridge took a different approach: while they used stronger bars than usual, they put only two in each bundle.

Over the years, the amount of bridge traffic and the weight of individual cars grew rapidly. On December 15,

Silver Bridge before the collapse

1967, during rush hour traffic, one of the eyebars gave out. The added stress on its companion eyebar was too much, and it, too, failed. The bridge collapsed, and 46 people fell to their deaths. Later analysis showed that the cause of the failure was a tiny defect, one-tenth of an inch or 2.5 mm deep, in the eye that had fractured.

Silver Bridge after the collapse

22 Five More Bridge Disasters (Bay Bridge, Sunshine Skyway, Big Bayou Canot, Winkley "Swinging" Bridge, Eschede)

Collapsed section of the Cypress Viaduct, Oakland

Earthquake: San Francisco-Oakland Bay Bridge, California, 1989

IT WAS OCTOBER 17, 1989. IN SAN FRANCISCO'S CANDLESTICK Park, the San Francisco Giants and Oakland A's were warming up for Game three of baseball's World Series. Because of the game, traffic was relatively light on the Bay Bridge when at 5:04 pm it began to roll in waves.

The cause was a magnitude 6.9 earthquake centered 60 miles away in the Santa Cruz mountains.

The Bay Bridge is a cantilever truss bridge with two decks carrying traffic in opposite directions. The Loma Prieta earthquake shifted the Oakland side of the bridge 7 inches (18 cm) to the east, shearing the bolts of a 250-ton section of the upper deck, which swung down and crashed against the lower deck. Amazingly, only one person was killed, when she drove her car into the gap that had suddenly appeared in the upper deck. Police spent hours redirecting traffic.

Elsewhere, the damage was much more severe. Worst of all was the Cypress Street Viaduct in West Oakland. The freeway, built of reinforced concrete and two levels high, was built on marshland. During the earthquake, the freeway twisted and buckled. Support columns collapsed, and the upper deck fell onto the lower deck, crushing drivers in their cars. Local people rushed to the rescue, carrying ladders; nearby factory workers brought forklifts. Rescuers managed to pull many survivors free of the wreckage, but in all, 42 people died.

Only the Loma Prieta earthquake is known to have caused a fatal bridge collapse.

Caltrans, the transit authority, rapidly repaired the Bay Bridge, re-opening it the following month. Reconstructing the Oakland freeway took much longer. Caltrans eventually rerouted the highway farther west, around the city. This rebuilding took almost twelve years. Meanwhile, in place of the old double-decker freeway, the state opened a street-level road named Mandela Parkway.

Ship collision: Sunshine Skyway Bridge, Florida, 1980

Ships can be dangerous to bridges. A barge or cargo ship can strike a bridge pier with enough force to make it collapse. In fact, there have been at least 36 such incidents in the past fifty years, with more than 340 deaths. Bad weather and poor visibility are often contributing factors.

One such accident brought down Florida's Sunshine Skyway Bridge over Tampa Bay in 1980. The Skyway was a four-lane truss bridge built on concrete piers. The morning of May 9 opened with a thunderstorm, but traffic crossed the bridge as usual.

In the shipping channel directly beneath the bridge, a sudden squall struck the freighter MV Summit Venture. The wind tore along at 70 mph, and rain

Sunshine Skyway Bridge with the ship that caused its collapse, 1980

fell in torrents. The pilot, who could hardly see, reversed his engines and dropped an anchor, trying to avoid disaster. But the swinging bow of the freighter struck two concrete piers, and a 1200-foot (370 m) span collapsed into the bay. Six cars, a truck, and a Greyhound bus fell with it. Thirty-five people died, but one man survived when his truck landed on the ship itself before slipping into the water.

No one on the ship was hurt.

Ship collision: Big Bayou Canot Bridge, Alabama, 1993

A similar accident, but with a twist, occurred in 1993 on the Big Bayou Canot Railway Bridge in southwestern Alabama. This time a boat went off course. In heavy fog, the pilot of a the towboat Mauvilla, pulling a string of six heavy barges, took a wrong turn off the Mobile River into a side bayou crossed by a rail bridge. At 2:45 a.m., navigating without a chart or compass and lacking proper training to read his radar, the pilot drove the Mauvilla into the bridge.

The structure had been designed as a swing bridge, though it had never been used as one. Still, the collision caused the "swinging" end of the bridge span to move about three feet (one meter) to the side. The track kinked but did not break, meaning no automatic signal was sent to stop any oncoming trains. At 2:53 a.m., the Amtrak train Sunset Limited approached the bridge at a speed of 70 mph (113 kph). Striking the kink, the head locomotive jumped the track, swung down, and crashed against the bridge substructure. Only then, struck by a falling locomotive, did the bridge collapse.

Fuel tanks exploded, engulfing the falling train in

Big Bayou Canot Bridge with the barge that struck it, 1993

oil and flames. Forty-two passengers died of the impact, injuries, smoke inhalation, burns, or drowning, while 103 suffered less serious injuries. The towboat's four crew members escaped unharmed.

Even today, Amtrak has not restored the passenger route between Orlando and New Orleans.

Poor maintenance and human folly: Winkley "Swinging" Bridge, Arkansas, 1996

The Winkley Bridge over the Little Red River in north central Arkansas was 77 years old the day it collapsed. Built in 1912, it was a suspension road bridge, with five-inch steel cables made of twisted wire. Suspended from wooden towers, the cables ran underneath the two sides of the wooden roadway. The bridge was 550 feet (170 m) long and ten feet wide. In 1944, the bridge's original wooden towers were replaced with steel.

In 1972, workers built a new bridge a few hundred feet downstream, and officials closed the Winkley bridge to vehicles. A team inspecting the bridge found a bit of rust on the outside of the steel cables, but none on the inside. The group pronounced the Winkley Bridge safe for pedestrians. However, the lead engineer did make two recommendations. First, the cables should be painted with a corrosive-resistant coating. Second, to be doubly sure they were safe, the cables should be examined by ultrasound. The county government did not follow either suggestion.

Pedestrians had a lot of fun with the Winkley Bridge. It had always swayed a little with traffic. Now young people found that when they all ran at once from one side to the other, laughing and squealing, they could make the bridge sway a little more. They nicknamed it "the swinging bridge."

On October 28, 1989, forty or fifty members of a church youth group gathered on the bridge. Soon they set it swaying in wider and wider arcs. It was too much. The cable under the upstream side of the bridge parted. The bridge tipped, increasing the tension on the second cable, which also snapped. The deck and all the pedestrians fell into the river below. Five people, including an 11-year-old child, died. Bystanders helped in the rescue, transporting the injured to local hospitals.

A later inspection of the cables showed that in some places, rust had penetrated all the way through.

Train derailment, Eschede, Germany, 1998

The world's worst high-speed train disaster occurred on June 3, 1998, in northern Germany. Sometime after 10:30 in the morning, Jöng Dittmann, a passenger in the first car, was startled when a shard of metal slashed through the floor, embedding itself in the armrest between his wife and child. Much later, investigators learned that this was the remainder of a steel tire that had peeled away from one of the train's wheels and flown upward.

Ushering his family out of the car, Dittman hurried to inform the conductor. By this time, the entire train was vibrating, but the conductor insisted on inspecting the damage before deciding whether to stop the train. As the two walked back to the first car, the train swayed side to side. Then the hanging piece of metal tire struck a guard rail at a switching site, launching the rail into the belly of the train. The train, which had been traveling at 200 km/h (120 mph), veered sideways. Its third car slammed into a concrete support pillar at one end of a road bridge passing overhead. This road bridge or overpass collapsed onto the rear cars of the train. The sixth car was crushed to a height of a few inches. The carriages behind it accordioned onto the pile of carriages ahead.

Clearing wreckage of the Eschede train disaster, 1998

More than a thousand rescue workers rushed to the site. They managed to extract all but one of the injured and get them to twenty-two different hospitals in a little over two hours. However, little could be done for those in the crushed carriages. In all, 101 people died, while a further 105 suffered injury.

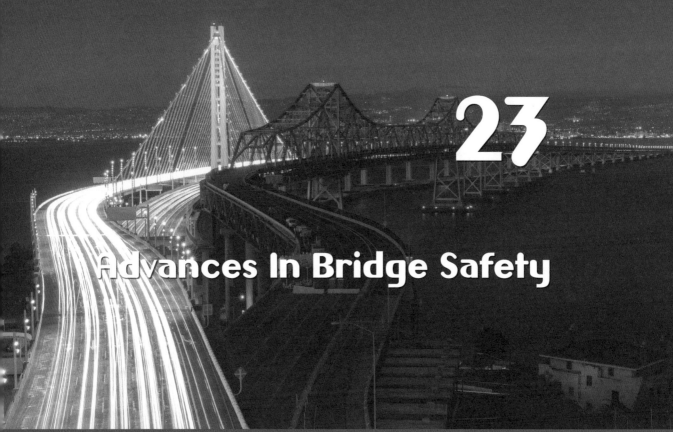

Eastern span of the San Francisco-Oakland Bay Bridge

23
Advances In Bridge Safety

Bridge engineers pay a lot of attention to safety. Starting in the 1800s, they began building models of bridges to test against various loads. Today, they have added computer modeling to physical models to simulate different conditions of wind, floods, ship collisions, earthquakes and other disasters.

When a bridge fails, engineers analyze the reasons and apply what they learn. After the Tay Bridge disaster, engineers began regularly testing models in wind tunnels and designing for much greater wind loads than before. They also mostly abandoned iron as a building material for longer bridges. To prevent another Tangiwai disaster, New Zealanders established an upstream warning system for lahars. The Tacoma Narrows bridge failure led engineers to design more aerodynamic bridges to allow wind to pass through or around the structure. And various ship collisions led bridge designers to add barriers and bollards standing some distance in front of bridge piers. These bollards can stop ships before they can collide with the piers or bridges themselves.

Today, examiners regularly inspect bridges for safety. In the United States, publicly managed bridges are inspected at least every two years. This schedule was established after the Silver Bridge disaster described in chapter 21.

Traditionally, inspectors have been engineering technicians who rely primarily on their eyes. First, they make sure all parts of the bridge are properly lined up, each piece in its appointed place. Then they look for rusting cables. They check for cracks in the roadway. Underneath, they take note of where concrete has crumbled. In such places, they check to see if the rebar within the concrete has been exposed to moisture. If it has, they estimate how much the reinforcing bars have been thinned by rust. Finally, they may even dive underwater to look for erosion or wear on bridge piers.

Bridge inspectors take photos, write up reports, and make recommendations. Structural engineers review the reports to determine a safe weight limit for each bridge. If the weight limit is too low for expected traffic, authorities close the bridge. If a bridge is starting to wear down, engineers schedule more frequent checkups.

Bridge Inspectors earn on average about $52,000 per year for a very important job. As we have seen in the previous two chapters, the lives of many travelers depend on their diligence.

Besides visually examining bridge components, inspectors may clean and scrape steel components, sound concrete segments, and use penetrating dyes to identify areas of cracking. Helpful technology includes echo and sound transmission systems, ground-penetrating radar and even X-rays.

Special sensors also help. Strain gauges convert pressure or tension into measurable changes in electrical resistance. Changes in current flow through the sensors signal that there is expansion or contraction. Accelerometers measure how much a bridge component moves in the wind or under the pressure of traffic.

Two advances in the technology of bridge safety are wireless sensors and drones. On the Penobscot River Bridge on page 119 or Amsterdam's new

3D printed steel bridge on page 174, sensors communicate wirelessly with monitoring stations. As for drones, it's far safer to have a drone fly around the top of a bridge tower than to have a human being trying to balance there. Drones can also use artificial intelligence to help them find cracks and zoom in for a better view.

24

Pedestrian Bridges
(London Millennium Footbridge,
Gateshead Millennium Bridge,
Zhangjiejiang Forest Glass Bridge,
Moses Bridge,
Bridges 2 Prosperity)

London Millennium Footbridge with St. Paul's Cathedral in the background

The earliest bridges were built for people on foot. Today, there are lots of pedestrian bridges that cross highways, rivers or gorges, allowing walkers to enjoy the beauty of their city or of wild places.

Millennium Footbridge, London, 2002

I N 1996, A CALL WENT OUT FOR DESIGNS FOR A pedestrian bridge over the river Thames. It would be London's first new bridge in more than a hundred years. Marking the new millennium, the new span would connect the city's financial center with Bankside, an art district that includes both the Tate Modern art museum and the new Globe Theater, which stands just 750 feet from the spot of Shakespeare's own theater. The judges called for a design that would neither block shipping nor disturb views of the city.

The selection committee chose a plan for a suspension bridge they described as "a blade of light." Designed by a sculptor and an architect, the bridge was to be built of steel, concrete and aluminum.

What is most remarkable about the bridge, completed in 2000, is its shallow profile. The aluminum bridge deck runs between the arms of two Y-shaped piers standing in the river. Eight steel suspension cables run from one Y to the other. Steel arms clamp onto the cables every eight meters to support the bridge deck. The cables never rise more than 2.3 meters (7.6 ft) above the walking surface, allowing walkers clear views of the river and the city. Strollers crossing from Bankside see the dome of St. Paul's cathedral straight ahead.

On opening day, June 10 2002, 80,000 people crossed the bridge, 2000 at a time. But immediately, a problem arose. The bridge's design allowed it to sway slightly from side to side. Each time it moved, people stepped sideways to catch themselves. Soon, 2000 people were stepping, then swaying, then staggering. The bridge oscillated wildly.

Worried authorities limited the number of people crossing at any one time. Lines grew long, visitors grumbled, and citizens called the whole structure a waste of money. And the bridge still swayed.

Officials closed the bridge two days after it opened. A scientific paper published later in *Nature* magazine explained what had happened. A flexible structure with a natural swaying frequency close to the pace of a human stride will necessarily sway more and more widely as people walk on it, adding their movements to its own. Without meaning to, as the bridge starts to sway,

Ben Williams at work

Natalie's Angel by Ben Williams

If you visit the Millennium Bridge today, you may find it sprinkled with tiny dots of color. The street painter Ben Wilson, sometimes called "The Chewing Gum Man," paints wads of gum stuck to the pavement with bright acrylic paints to create miniature works of art. It's a creative idea—turning litter into art!

people stagger in time with it. Scientists calculated that as few as 160 pedestrians could cause the bridge to swing more and more wildly.

To solve the problem, engineers added 91 vertical and lateral dampers, both viscous dampers like the shock absorbers used in cars and tuned mass dampers, which are heavy masses stiffened by springs. After testing, the bridge re-opened in February 2002. Although it was now stable, Londoners still called it "the wobbly bridge."

Gateshead Millennium Bridge, Newcastle, England, 2001

London was not the only English city to celebrate the millennium with a new pedestrian bridge. The northern industrial city of Newcastle also held a design contest, for a bridge across the River Tyne. Like London's Millennium Bridge, this one, too, would allow river traffic to pass and would not obstruct views of the city's other bridges.

The winners designed a curved, tilting, movable bridge for cyclists and pedestrians. A steel arch bridge 413 feet (126 m) long, it cost 22 million pounds to build. Construction workers set piers 30 feet into the ground. Steel sections of the bridge, built off site, came to Newcastle, where workers welded and painted them. Then a giant floating crane, the Asian Hercules II, carried the entire structure six miles upriver. On November 20, 2001, the crane lifted the bridge into place.

Newcastle's Millennium Bridge actually consists of two arches joined at their bases. When the bridge deck is down, one arch provides a curved path across the river, while the top of the other arch rises 50 meters above the roadway. Viewed end on, the two arches form the edges of a giant V lying on one side.

When the bridge needs to move to allow a boat to pass, an alarm rings. People on the deck hurry off. Eight electric motors then turn a pivot at the end of the bridge, and the entire structure tilts backward by 40 degrees. The arch that forms the bridge deck rotates upward as the upper arch rotates back and down.

You can watch all this happen on YouTube.

In motion, the whole structure has the look of a blinking eye, leading some to call it the "Winking Eye Bridge." As it tilts, the bridge cleans up any litter, which rolls into traps along the edge of the bridge deck.

The bridge tilted for the first time on June 28, 2001. Opening or closing it takes just 4 1/2 minutes and is so energy-efficient that the cost of each opening is only four pounds, or about five dollars. At night, the entire structure is lit with hundreds of three-watt LED lights, all carefully directed to minimize light pollution. While on weeknights the lights are white, on weekends they switch to festive, colored patterns.

Gateshead Millennium Bridge. On the right, the bridge is raised and a ship sails under.

If heights make you nervous, this is not the bridge for you.

Zhangjiajie Forest Glass Bridge, Hunan, China, 2016

How would you like to walk on glass 300 meters (1,000 ft) above the forest floor? That experience greets visitors to the Zhangjiajie Forest in Hunan province in central China. The bridge is found in a national park in Wulingyuan, which is famous for the sandstone quartzite pillars thrusting upward among its trees. The location is one of several that inspired James Cameron as he created the landscape for his film *Avatar*.

The Zhangjiajie Bridge is a steel suspension bridge designed by the Israeli poet and professor Haim Dotan. The two towers of the bridge,

Zhangjiejiang Forest Glass Bridge

anchored in rock on either side of a canyon, rise 60 meters into the air. Steel suspension cables support a bridge deck built of thick glass plates fourteen meters wide. Fearless tourists walk and skip across the bridge, looking down at three long swings that hang beneath it and anticipating the day officials decide to launch the highest bungee jump in the world.

The great glass bridge was constructed to carry 800 walkers safely at any one time. But that turned out not to be enough. Just thirteen days after opening, officials closed the bridge because of overwhelming crowds. They had expected 8000 visitors a day; instead they found themselves facing 80,000. Suddenly they had to upgrade parking, ticketing lines, and techniques for safely managing large crowds.

Tourists still flock to the bridge today, though they sometimes complain about the long lines, the crowds, and the cost of tickets. Worse, there are reports that the glass surface itself is becoming scratched and scuffed, which interferes with the view.

China has since built an even longer glass bridge in the Hongyagu scenic area in Hebei, northern China. With a span of 149 meters (489 ft) across a canyon, the Hongyagu glass bridge links two mountain peaks. The glass panels that make up the glass deck are about as thick as your thumb is long. Visitors to this newer bridge are required to wear "shoe gloves" to keep from scratching the glass.

Moses Bridge (Fort de Roovere), Netherlands, 2010

How about a bridge you can't even see, an "invisible" bridge?

A modest and unusual pedestrian bridge can be found in the village of Hasteren in the Netherlands. The bridge allows visitors to cross a moat to the 17th century Fort de Roovere.

Much of the western Netherlands lies below sea level. Strong earthen dikes protect land that was reclaimed from the sea centuries ago. In the 17th century, the Netherlands began its Eighty Years' War for independence from Spain. Outnumbered and desperate to protect their northern provinces from invading French and Spanish armies, the Dutch breached the dikes, allowing water to flow across broad swaths of land to obstruct the advancing soldiers. Fort de Roovere lay at a key point in the West Brabant Line of forts built above the swamps and flooded land. Its guns were aimed at the few dikes that still rose above water to connect the small towns and fortresses.

More than once in the decades that followed, armies that tried to invade found themselves floundering in mud and water up to their waists. Spikes planted underwater could pierce an infantryman's belly. The water between forts was too deep for armies to march through, but it was also too shallow for their ships to navigate.

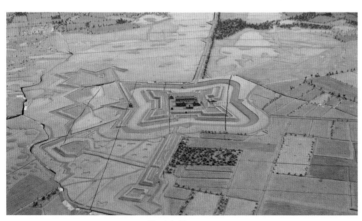

Fort de Roovere

The West Brabant Line held against the French army in 1672, but the fields remained flooded for almost a century. When lasting peace finally arrived, the Dutch built up their dikes again and drained the swamps and low waterways. They opened the land to agriculture once more. Gradually, abandoned forts fell into disrepair.

Then, at the beginning of the 21st century, the Dutch government decided to recreate the line of forts and dikes, connecting them with biking and hiking paths. A moat protected one side of Fort de Roovere. Authorities wanted a bridge to cross it without disturbing the fort's air of watery isolation.

Bridge designers came up with a unique solution. They built an "invisible" bridge—a deep, wooden furrow through the moat. Descending a series of steps, visitors seem to disappear into the water as they venture onto a bridge deck several feet below the moat's surface. Wooden walls holding back the water rise only an inch or two above water level. People crossing can trail their fingers in the ripples.

The bridge is built of specially treated wood expected to last fifty years. Dams on either end of the moat control the water level to keep it from overflowing the wooden trench. And because it seems to part the waters as Moses did at the Red Sea, the bridge is nicknamed the "Moses Bridge."

Kurilpa Footbridge, Brisbane, Australia, 2009

The Kurilpa footbridge, which crosses the Brisbane River in Queensland, Australia, opened in 2009. It has a fascinating design. Six and a half meters wide and 470 meters (1,500 ft) long, it is held up by a jumble of 20 steel masts and 16 horizontal spans that together look like a giant heap of knitting needles. Though the knitting needles appear to stick out randomly in all directions, they are actually carefully arranged according to the principles of **tensegrity**.

Masts of the Kurilpa Bridge

Tensegrity was named and developed as a concept by the architect Buckminster Fuller. It's short for "tensional integrity;" some people speak instead of "floating compression." Whatever the name, the underlying principle is that every structural member is under either pure tension or pure compression. Bars that are under compression don't touch. Instead, they're suspended within a net under continual tension.

Maybe you've seen a tensegrity sculpture and wondered what can possibly be holding it up! Designing a tensegrity structure takes a lot of math and physics knowledge.

This is a free-standing tensegrity structure.

Needle Tower by Kenneth Snelson, Hirschorn Sculpture Garden

The Kurilpa bridge has two large platforms where pedestrians can pause and view the river. An all-weather canopy shades walkers from hot sun and protects them from pouring rain. For illumination, the bridge use light-emitting diodes (LEDs), and 75 to 100 percent of its energy needs come from solar power.

Bridges to Prosperity

The pedestrian bridges we've talked about so far in this chapter are tourist attractions and conveniences. But in the developing world, footbridges can be lifelines, connecting people to schools, markets, and medical clinics. Here's a charity that makes a huge difference in people's lives by literally building bridges!

In May 2001, Kenneth Frantz, the owner of a construction business, saw a photograph in *National Geographic* magazine. The photo showed men trying to cross a broken stone arch bridge over the Blue Nile in Ethiopia. So desperate were people to cross the river that they were boosting one another along a rope strung precariously across the gap.

The photograph reminded Frantz how important bridges could be to people in isolated villages. With the help of family, colleagues, and the local Rotary Club, he donated time and money to repair the bridge in the photograph. That was just the start. Soon Frantz enrolled Zoe Keone Pacciani and Chris Rollins as co-founders of a charity they called Bridges to Prosperity (B2P). Together, they designed a program to build suspension bridges while training community members in construction. The program brings together donors, volunteers, local communities, and local and national governments to tackle the problem of rural isolation.

B2P starts every new project by examining a local community's needs. Sometimes villagers have to walk miles out of their way to cross a river, meaning that it takes hours for children to get to school, for their parents to carry goods to market, or for families to take sick relatives to the doctor. Sometimes an existing river crossing may be safe during the dry season but dangerous when the rains come and the river rises.

Next, B2P examines local resources. What materials can be found close at hand or bought locally? What needs to be donated from abroad? Who in the community can help with planning and building? Are the local and national government supportive? Once it knows the answers, the B2P team designs a suspension bridge that fits the site and uses available resources. Industry volunteers who are skilled construction workers help to teach local people how to build the bridge. Instead of bulldozers, cattle and donkeys may move earth and equipment.

The average B2P bridge costs about $60,000 to build and takes about eight weeks to complete. Once a bridge is in place, professionals return every couple of years to inspect it for safety.

In this way, B2P has built over 250 durable pedestrian bridges serving over a million people in 22 countries, including Rwanda, Panama, Nicaragua, Haiti, and Bolivia. Motorcycles, bicycles, farm animals and walkers cross the bridges. Children get to school on time, the sick and elderly get to medical care, and goods get to market. B2P studies show that the average family using one of the new bridges sees its income rise by almost a third.

Currently, Bridges to Prosperity is run by a young woman named Avery Bang who started out as a volunteer. The charity raises and spends between $2 and $6 million annually. By 2020, they hope to be building 200 bridges each year.

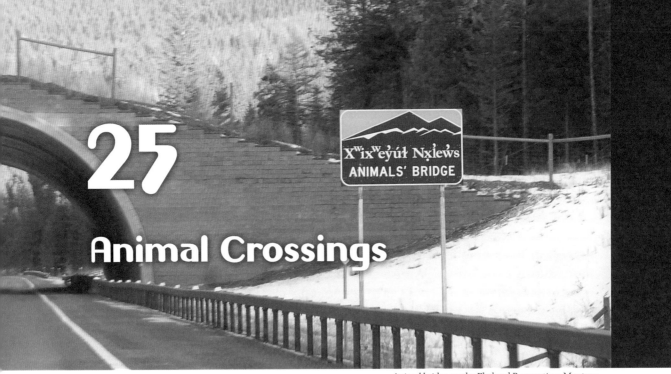

25

Animal Crossings

Animal bridge on the Flathead Reservation, Montana

ONE WHOLE CLASS OF BRIDGES ISN'T MEANT FOR HUMANS to cross at all. Instead, these bridges protect wildlife by providing ways for animals to cross highways in safety.

Highways and roads often cut right through animal habitats. They may interrupt migration pathways or divide the range where a species lives into areas too small to support a healthy population. In search of food or mates,

Key deer

animals wander onto these roads and highways, and each year, hundreds of thousands become roadkill.

In fact, the Federal Highway Administration lists 21 species in the U.S. whose very survival is threatened by collisions with vehicles on roads and highways. These include Florida panthers, Alabama red-bellied turtles, bighorn sheep, Key deer, many amphibians, and even birds.

Hitting a large animal with a car is also expensive and dangerous for the driver and any passengers.

Colliding with a moose costs on average $44,600 in car repairs and medical bills. One estimate puts the annual cost of animal-vehicle collisions in the U.S. at $8 billion a year. So what can be done to keep both drivers and animals safe?

One answer is wildlife crossings. These can be overpasses or underpasses, viaducts or tunnels. Whatever their form, we can think of them as bridges—spans that safely cross an expanse and an obstacle, in this case a road or highway if not a river or gorge.

The French built the first animal bridges in 1950. Today, to figure out where to put a passageway, wildlife biologists examine migration paths and areas of frequent collisions. Once an underpass or overpass is ready, highway workers build fences to funnel animals toward the safe crossing point.

In general, bridges at least 50 meters wide are needed for herd animals, like deer or elk, or large animals that like a lot of open space, like grizzly bears or wild boar. Underpasses attract smaller animals or those that want cover, like black bears in Canada, golden lion tamarin monkeys in Brazil, and water voles (small, mouse-like rodents) in London. In North America, even trout and salamanders may use watery underpasses.

Golden lion tamarin

In order to attract animals to use a bridge or overpass, conservation groups plant it with native grasses or shrubs. However, they keep the crossing a bit sparse. They don't want to make so attractive that, for example, a herd of elk lingers for days, because their presence may discourage other animals from crossing.

Once a passageway is ready, scientists can measure how many animals cross it by analyzing webcam video or counting animal tracks. They have learned that some species are slow to start using bridges. For example, starting in 2014, wildlife biologists studied how animals used bridges in the mountains of Washington State. Deer, elk, coyotes, mountain lions, and pika all began using bridges not long after they were put in

Pika are related to rabbits, but they have shorter, roundish ears and no visible tail.

American pika

Wolverine

Orangutans at the D.C. Zoo

place. Other animals, such as lynx, wolverines, and fishers, took up to five years before first daring to make the crossing. But once they started, they brought along their young, which means knowledge of the crossing will be passed down through the generations.

A 50-meter wide wildlife bridge might cost $2 to $4 million to build and landscape. Underpasses usually cost only one tenth as much. Then there are even simpler solutions. A rope bridge across a highway may be sufficient for squirrels or monkeys. The National Zoo in Washington, D.C. encourages orangutans to cross from one enclosure to another along a rope walkway above the heads of the tourists below.

Orangutans at the D.C. Zoo

No animal bridges get more use than the red crab bridges of Christmas Island in the Indian Ocean. Forty to fifty million red crabs live on the island, and in October or November of each year they migrate from the highlands to the ocean to breed. Year after year, thousands of them have been crushed as they crossed roads on their way.

To stop the smelly carnage, authorities built both tunnels and bridges. Now walls along the edges of the roads direct the crabs to the crossing points. The bridges offer nearly vertical climbs of steel mesh, but the crabs swarm across them without trouble, clacking and clattering overhead while cars pass smoothly below.

Wildlife bridges protect biodiversity. They do much more than saving individual animals from accidental death. Passageways increase a population's range, so animals can find food even in hard times. Most importantly, they allow subpopulations to mix, so small groups don't become inbred. A larger gene pool gives a population greater

Baby red crabs on Christmas Island

variation. This diversity means better resistance to disease and more ability to adapt to changes in the environment.

North America
black bear, coyote, fisher, grizzly, deer, elk, mountain goat, pika, squirrel, pronghorn, toads, salamander, trout, lynx, mountain lion, wolf, wolverine, bobcat (from top left, clockwise)

South America
puma, jaguar, golden lion tamarin

Here are some of the animals that use animal bridges and underpasses, by continent

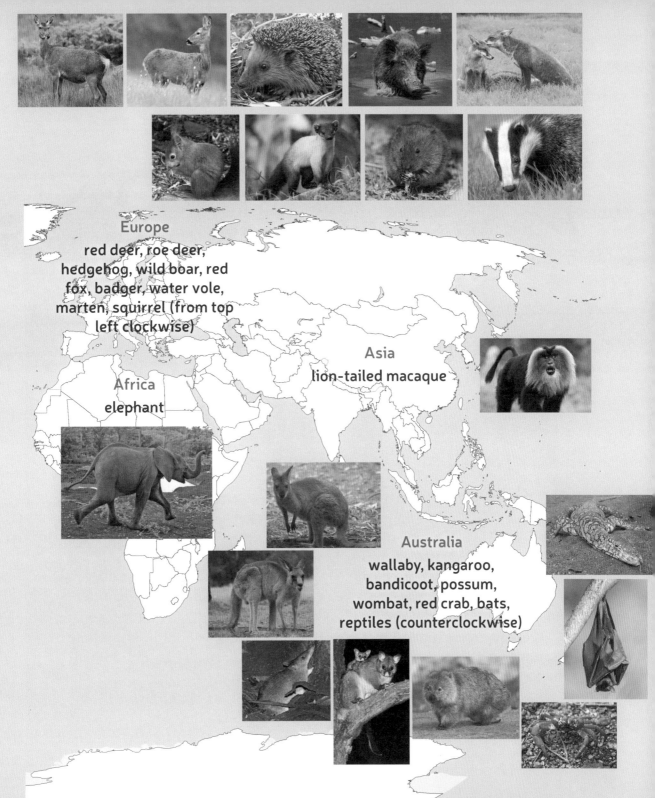

Europe

red deer, roe deer, hedgehog, wild boar, red fox, badger, water vole, marten, squirrel (from top left clockwise)

Asia

lion-tailed macaque

Africa

elephant

Australia

wallaby, kangaroo, bandicoot, possum, wombat, red crab, bats, reptiles (counterclockwise)

26

Sustainable Design and Construction

Bridge under construction in Kiev, Ukraine

What makes a bridge green?

IN RECENT YEARS, ENGINEERS HAVE BEEN working to design bridges that are friendly to the environment. A sustainable bridge safely crosses an expanse while limiting how much land it uses and how much it disturbs the view. It avoids harm to rare plants or animals. It's affordable to build, run, maintain and repair. The bridge allows people to cross in different ways, by car or light rail, by bicycle or on foot.

Perhaps most importantly, a sustainable bridge is built to last a long time. A bridge that lasts 100 years does much less harm to the environment than a bridge that has to be replaced every 30 years.

Sustainable or green design also means thinking about how a bridge affects the climate. Is it built of materials that release tons of CO_2 into the atmosphere, contributing to global warming? Or can the bridge be built of recycled or renewable materials? Does it shorten commute times so people end up driving less than before? Does it encourage people to walk, ride bicycles or use light rail instead of cars? How much energy is needed to run the bridge?

Some bridges can serve more than one purpose. Can solar panels or windmills on the bridge actually generate energy? Can plants grow on it or people live on it?

Futuristic bridge designs

New shapes

Every year, design contests around the world allow architecture firms to put forward their most daring bridge ideas. Fantastic shapes, multiple uses, and energy efficiency are emerging themes.

For example, in 2014 the architecture firm Sanzport won a design award for its Dynamic Shape-Shifting Helical Bridge, or DSSH. The bridge is meant to be a pedestrian bridge between two office towers. The proposed bridge would be modular, so the same design could easily be expanded and fitted to different sites. A frame of carbon fiber tubes would allow flexibility in case the buildings sway in slightly different directions. Solar panels would unfold to provide clean energy for fantastic LED lighting. Plants would flank the walkway to provide users with fresh, clean air.

Shape-shifting helical bridges sound amazing, but so far, nobody has offered to build one.

Habitable bridges

Another idea hovering in the air is the notion of habitable bridges—bridges where people can live and work. In Renaissance times, the Ponte Vecchio was lined with shops; in the 1700s people still lived on London Bridge. As Mark Twain described it in *The Prince and the Pauper*, the bridge

> . . . was a curious affair, for a closely packed rank of stores and shops, with family quarters overhead, stretched along both sides of it, from one bank of the river to the other. The Bridge

was a sort of town to itself; it had its inn, its beer-houses, its bakeries, its haberdasheries, its food markets, its manufacturing industries, and even its church. . . . Children were born on the Bridge, were reared there, grew to old age . . .

No modern bridge has yet been built to rival the old London Bridge. But for Expo 2008, Zaha Hadid designed a bridge in Zaragoza, Spain, that contains a large pavilion for exhibitions. Covered in triangles made from concrete reinforced with fiberglass, the bridge has an almost reptilian skin. The 280-meter (920-ft) bridge allowed 10,000 visitors to enter the Expo park every hour. After the Expo ended, a local bank bought the bridge to use for special shows.

In Mexico City, a firm called BNKR Arquitectura has publicized a design for a habitable bridge. The bridge would be 3 km long. The main deck would carry traffic, saving a long, jammed drive around the bay, while pedestrians and bicyclists would use a second level. Surrounding the core roadway, triangular structures would hold luxury apartments. Gardens and parks would cover the roofs, and escalators would lead down to docks for visiting yachts, tour boats, or vessels delivering whatever the inhabitants might want.

It's hard to build new bridges because they cost so much. BNKR architects argue that condos on the bridge, overlooking the bay, could attract such high prices that selling or leasing them could help make the bridge pay for itself.

Zaragoza pavilion bridge

Recycled building materials

Concrete, the world's most commonly used material for building bridges, has a huge impact on the environment. Converting limestone into cement for concrete releases nearly a ton of CO_2 into the atmosphere for every ton of concrete created. Then, when a building or bridge is demolished, broken-up concrete sits in landfill, useless.

People have looked at the possibility of recycling concrete. Some towns use chunks of broken concrete as riprap, which is stone installed for retaining walls or along the banks of rivers to help prevent erosion. Crunched-up concrete can also be mixed into new concrete. To maintain strength in the new concrete, no more than 30 percent of it should come from recycled pieces.

Steel can also be recycled. When an old steel bridge needs to be demolished, its steel members can be cut into short lengths and returned to a factory to be melted down and re-used. Unlike concrete, recycled steel loses none of its strength.

Although steel and concrete remain the strongest and most versatile materials for building bridges, some cities and towns are trying recycled plastic. In the U.S., we recycle less than 30 percent of hard plastic waste, so there's plenty left over. Plastic beams can be built from shredded laundry detergent bottles and milk cartons. Fiberglass is mixed in for added strength. Plastic I-beams cost less and are much lighter than concrete or steel. And unlike wood, plastic resists rot, moisture, and insects. Plastic bridges are expected to last over a hundred years.

For now, plastic bridges are short. In 2011, the plastic Birch Hill Road Bridge opened in York, Maine. Fifteen feet (5 m) long, it carries both cars and pedestrians. 2013 brought the 24.6-foot (7.5-m) Onion Ditch Bridge of West Liberty, Ohio. Scotland builds longer plastic bridges. In December 2011, the Easter Dawyck Bridge opened over Scotland's River Tweed. The first recycled plastic bridge in Europe, it has three spans and a total length of 90 feet (27 m). It used 20 tons of recycled plastic and can carry a load of up to 45 tons (40 tonnes).

Easter Dawyck Bridge, Scotland, built of recycled plastic

Even the U.S. Army has experimented with plastic bridges. Some of the recycled plastic bridges it has built on military bases have load ratings of 73 to 130 tons.

Canals crisscross the port city of Rotterdam in the Netherlands. As some of its 850 pedestrian bridges wear out, the city is replacing them with fiber-reinforced polymer (FRP)—basically plastic. The first FRP bridge was installed in 2009. By 2016, there were 90 of them. Today, a light, prefabricated plastic bridge over a canal can be installed in less than an hour.

27

New Materials and Methods

P LASTICS ARE NOT THE ONLY NEW MATERIALS BRIDGE
builders are using. We've already talked about some pedestrian bridges with
decks made of glass. Bridge engineers are also experimenting with organic
materials, new safety monitoring devices, and even 3D printing.

New materials

Glulam is short for glued laminated timber. Light, strong, and long-
lasting, glulam consists of many layers of wood bonded together with wa-
ter-resistant glues. In each layer, the grain of the wood runs parallel to the

long axis of the glulam board or beam. Glulam is used for posts, horizontal beams, and even curved shapes such as arches.

Glulam weighs one-tenth as much as steel and one-sixth as much as cement. Manufacturing it requires less energy and emits less carbon than manufacturing either concrete or steel. Computers can control how glulam is cut and shaped into precise, complex curves. This means less wood is wasted than with traditional wooden beams.

Sports arenas often use glulam in their roofs, because it can arch over long expanses without the need for columns to hold up the middle. Glulam is also used for bridges—forest and pedestrian bridges, but also bridges carrying vehicles and trains. An example is this Apple Valley Road Bridge over a creek in Lyons, Colorado.

Apple Valley glulam bridge

Glulam does have a couple of disadvantages. For one, the glue used to make it comes from petroleum, which is not a renewable resource. Second, the material tends to be brittle, not as ductile as steel.

More recently, a researcher named Yan Xiao has extended the glulam concept to bamboo. **Glubam** consists of laminated lengths of bamboo fiber. Bamboo is a rapidly renewable resource, and growing it draws carbon dioxide from the air. Manufacturing glubam takes little energy compared to manufacturing concrete and steel, so it is an environmentally friendly building material. Active research continues to investigate the properties of glubam structures, including their strength and how well they hold up over multiple cycles of moisture and dryness.

In 2007, Dr. Xiao's team built a 10-meter bridge in Leiyang, Hunan, China. Assembling the bridge took only ten days, and when finished, it could bear loads of up to 8 tons.

Bio-composites are materials that include a mix of polymers whose origin is living things. For example, bio-composites may mix hemp, cotton, or flax fiber with sticky resins from other plants. Bio-composites' strength comes from the number and strength of the natural fibers they contain.

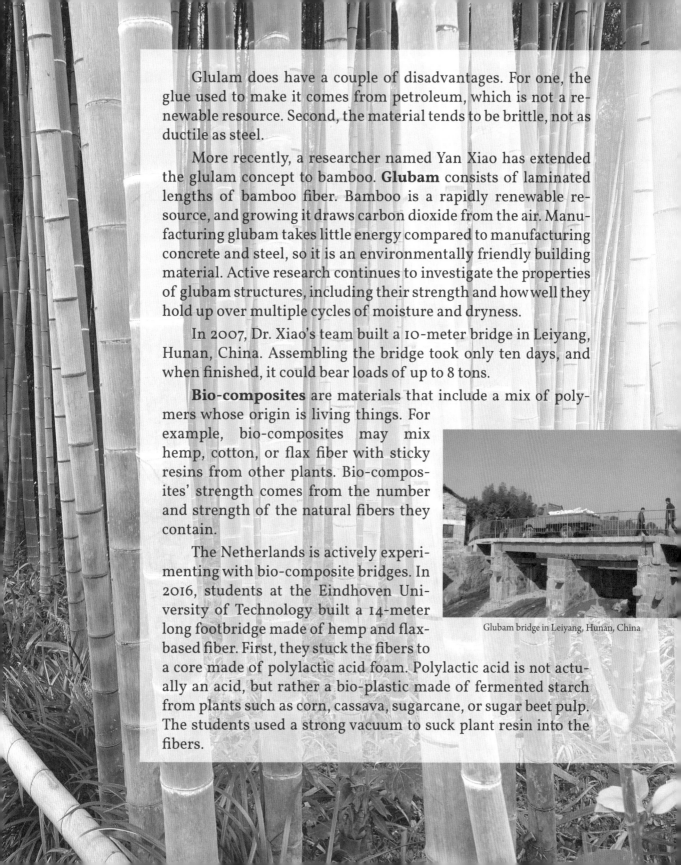

Glubam bridge in Leiyang, Hunan, China

The Netherlands is actively experimenting with bio-composite bridges. In 2016, students at the Eindhoven University of Technology built a 14-meter long footbridge made of hemp and flax-based fiber. First, they stuck the fibers to a core made of polylactic acid foam. Polylactic acid is not actually an acid, but rather a bio-plastic made of fermented starch from plants such as corn, cassava, sugarcane, or sugar beet pulp. The students used a strong vacuum to suck plant resin into the fibers.

After this successful trial, the Dutch have begun to build other bio-composite bridges, for pedestrians, bicycles, and even cars. Some of these new bridges, such as a folding bridge at the Wildlands Adventure Zoo in Emmen, combine bio-composites with small amounts of recycled plastic bottles and even tiny amounts of steel.

One advantage of bio-composites is that they are ultimately biodegradable. This means they can be disposed of without harm to the environment. But might they biodegrade in place? How well bio-composites stand up to the normal wear of weather and time is still under study.

Bacterial cement

What if you could get bacteria to grow cement? Scientists have been working on this trick for over twenty years. One expert on bacterial cement is Ginger Krieg Dosier, an American professor in the United Arab Emirates. Inspired by how coral reefs grow, she developed a process for "growing" bricks. The process involves placing sand in molds and adding *Sporosacina pasteurii* bacteria, then feeding them calcium ions suspended in water.

Ginger Krieg Dosier

Growing a brick with bacteria takes two to five days, about the same as the three to five days it takes to bake a brick in a kiln. However, firing bricks in a kiln requires heating them to 2000 °F (1100 degrees C). This heating uses lots of energy.

Dosier has formed a company to start manufacturing her bricks in large numbers. She also licenses the technology to other companies. Her dream is to replace as many as possible of the 1.2 trillion bricks manufactured every year. This way, she hopes to make a dent in the 800 million tons of carbon released into the atmosphere by brick-building each year.

Meanwhile, other scientists are studying the use of *Sporosacina* and other urea-splitting bacteria as additives to enhance the durability of bricks and mortar. The material can even be sprayed onto concrete surfaces to help "heal" cracks and protect breakdown. The bacteria start to build tiny columns of limestone to fill the gap. As a protective coating, the bacteria-based mixture can help concrete structures remain safe longer. This is of special interest for maintaining monuments and historical structures.

Electron micrograph of concrete "healing" over a crack

New methods

Besides new materials, architects and engineers are experimenting with new methods of construction.

To me it looks like a giant, clumsy cake decoration made of squeezed-out white frosting.

One of the most surprising is scaled-up 3D printing. In December 2016, the Institute for Advanced Architecture of Catalonia (IAAC) installed the world's first 3D printed bridge in a park outside of Madrid, Spain. The footbridge, 12 meters (39 ft) by 1.75 m (5.7 ft), is made of micro-reinforced concrete, with steel mesh embedded at a few key points.

U.S. Marines have printed a concrete bridge in place in Fort Pendleton, California. While in no way beautiful, the bridge works. Moreover, it suggests that Marine Corps engineers will eventually be able to build durable bridges and other structures quickly for disaster relief and military uses.

3D printed concrete bridge near Madrid, Spain

Dutch designer Joris Laarman is the first to try building a bridge of 3D-printed steel. Robotic arms crawled out along the length of the bridge as they built it by dripping molten steel. As one member of the team described the experience, it was "like drawing in mid-air." Originally, Laarman hoped to build the bridge right in place across a canal in central Amsterdam. However, safety concerns (What if curious passersby got burned by the molten

3D printed concrete bridge at Fort Pendleton, California

metal?) led authorities to advise that the bridge be built inside the factory warehouse.

Four robots took six months to complete their task: a finished bridge 12 meters (39 ft) long by 4 meters (13 ft) wide. Along its length, a smart network of embedded sensors transmits information about strain, displacement, vibration, temperature, and even air quality. In October 2018, the bridge was displayed at Dutch Design Week, where it won a prize. The judges declared, "The form and material freedom achieved by Laarman [...] hint at almost unimaginable scenarios." The dripped-steel bridge is scheduled to be installed over the canal in 2019.

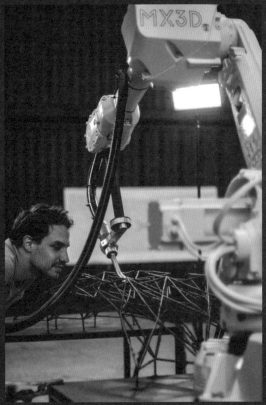

Stages of construction, 3D printed steel bridge, MX3D, the Netherlands

28

Bridges Yesterday, Today, and Tomorrow

W E'VE COME TO THE END OF our tour of the world's most intriguing bridges. There are so many more I could show you—but we have to stop somewhere!

What I hope you've seen is that for hundreds, even thousand of years, people have been seeking better ways to cross gaps. They've discovered or invented new materials. They've imagined new designs. And even as they challenged themselves to span deeper gorges and wider bays, engineers have paid special attention to beauty and safety.

Bridge to Mars, Yards Park, Washington, D.C.

Building safer, stronger, longer bridges has required advances in materials, design, and construction methods. It has also responded to new demands. A bridge that stands up to chariots might well crumble under the weight of a freight train.

The first bridges, logs, could cross gaps no wider than the length of a tree trunk. Once builders began quarrying stone, they invented the arch, which allowed them to build tall, wide, durable bridges that held themselves together. Still, the weight of stone bridges limited how high they could be built. And the only way to construct arches was by setting stones in place over supporting structures of wood built up from the ground. That made it hard to cross deep or rapid rivers.

The smelting of iron and manufacture of steel provided materials that made bridges stronger. At the same time, the great weight of these metals spurred the development of new, lighter designs with more free space. Components could be manufactured offsite and then brought by barge or train or truck to the bridge site. Iron and steel could be shaped into new forms, such as a bowstring arch. The length and strength of steel members made new construction techniques possible, like cantilevering pre-built pieces over wide expanses. Cantilevering allowed metal arch or girder bridges to be built without wooden scaffolding underneath.

New designs allowed wood, along with iron and steel, to be used in new ways. Trusses helped to distribute the load on a bridge. I-beams and box girders allowed builders to use great lengths of steel while keeping weight down.

Suspension bridges are an old technology, used by Tibetans in the Himalayas and Incas in the Andes. Iron chain links or woven grass both served for suspension bridges. But to build such landmarks as the Brooklyn Bridge, the Golden Gate and the Akashi Kaikyo Bridge, engineers needed to build models and make careful calculations of what wind, weight, tides or earthquakes might do. Building these bridges also required advances in construction technique—the use of caissons to build foundations underwater and spun steel wire for cables.

Cement has been used since at least Roman times. But before it could be used for long bridges, concrete had to be reinforced with steel. Today concrete shows up in girders that cross wide expanses and in bridges that continue to break records for length.

Through the centuries, engineers have continued to learn about safety. It used to be accepted that a certain number of workers would inevitably die during the construction of a new bridge. Today, nets, safety harnesses, hard hats, weather monitoring, and careful modeling protect workers on the job. Accidents still happen. Winds, floods, collisions, earthquakes, and aging still cause some bridges to fail. But the vast majority of bridges stand strong year after year. And after each disaster or near-disaster, engineers analyze the cause and use their new knowledge to make tomorrow's bridges safer.

Today's engineers devote ever more attention to making their bridges not only beautiful but sustainable. That means experimenting with new materials, including plastics, composite polymers, and even cement made by bacteria. It means exploring prefabricated bridges and bridges made by robots using 3D printing. It also means coming up with daring new designs that minimize energy use and encourage people to walk or ride bicycles. These designs may even include plantings and places for people to live.

Perhaps someday, we can apply the same level of vision and thought to building friendships between countries as we do to constructing physical bridges. Meantime, people won't stop building. We'll strive for beauty, safety, and strength. We'll look for ways to cross gaps that seem impossible to cross. Lately I've been wondering: What kind of bridges will we build across the great canyons of Mars?

Valles Marineris, Mars

Chronological Table of Bridges

Bridge Name	Year completed	Country	Barrier crossed	Overall length
Arkadiko	13th c. BC - Greek Bronze Age	Ancient Greece	gully	a few meters
Xerxes' Pontoon Bridge	480 B.C	Asia-Europe	Hellespont	about 1.6 km
Pont du Gard	First century	France	Gardon R.	275 m
Segovia Aqueduct	between 96 and 112	Spain	crosses land	16 km, in sections
Alcántara	106	Spain	Tagus R.	182 m
Anji (Zhaozhou)	Sui Dynasty, around 700 CE	China	Xiaohe R.	51 m
Dongjin pontoon bridge	Song dynasty (960-1269 CE)	China	Gong R.	about 400 m
Q'iswa Chaka	1300s to now	Peru	Apurimac R.	30 m
Kapellbrücke (Chapel)	1333	Switzerland	R. Reuss	204 m
Ponte Vecchio	1345	Italy, Florence	Arno R.	84 m
Chakzam	1422?	Tibet	Yarlung Tsangpo	137 m?
Rialto	1591	Italy, Venice	Grand Canal	32 m
Si-o-se-pol	1602	Iran, Isfahan	Zayanderud	295 m
Mathematical Bridge	1749	England, Cambridge	Cam R.	12 m
Iron Bridge	1781	England , Shropshire	Severn R.	60 m

Style	Material used	Comments	Page
corbel arch	stone	used by chariots; precursor to true arch	23
pontoon	wooden ships	For invading Persian army, as described by Herodotus	32
true arch	stone	three levels with aqueduct	29
true arch aqueduct	stone	two levels	27
true arch	stone	three levels; built using cofferdams	25
segmented arch	stone	only 87 degrees of arch; open spandrels for water flow	36
pontoon	wooden planks and boats	about 100 wooden boats, still present and used today	33
suspension	ichu grass	woven grass rope bridge rebuilt each year	20
covered bridge	wood	17th c. paintings under roof	46
arches, closed spandrel	stone	shops along the bridge, Vasari corridor	38
suspension	iron chain links	built by Buddhist monk; one of first iron bridges, iron forged locally	57
segmental arch	stone	single span, designed by Antonia da Ponte	40
Safavid arches	stone	33 lower arches, two levels, pedestrian bridge	41
tangent and radial truss	wood	straight beams look curved; not built by Isaac Newton	48
arch	cast iron	single span, first iron bridge in the west	56

Bridge Name	Year completed	Country	Barrier crossed	Overall length
Pont-y-Cafnau	1793	Wales	Taff R.	14 m
Ponte das Barcas	1806	Portugal	Douro R.	130 -170 m?
Living root bridges	1844	India and Indonesia	many	shortish
Britannia Railway Bridge	1850	Wales	Menai Strait	461 m
Göltzsch Viaduct	1851	Germany	Göltzsch Valley	574 m
Bow Bridge	1862	USA, NYC	The Lake, Central Park	26.5 m
Eads Bridge	1869	St. Louis	Mississippi R.	1964 m
Tay Bridge	1878	Scotland	Firth of Tay	3000 m
Brooklyn Bridge	1883	USA, NYC	East R.	1825 m
Niagara Cantilever	1883	USA/Canada	Niagara R.	27.4 m
Queen Emma Bridge	1888	Curaçao	St. Anna Bay	167 m
Forth Railway Bridge	1890	Scotland	Firth of Forth	2529 m
Tower Bridge	1894	England, London	Thames	244 m
Tavanasa Bridge	1904	Switzerland	Rhine R.	50 m
Victoria Falls Bridge	1905	Zambia/ Zimbabwe	Zambezi R.	205 m

Style	Material used	Comments	Page
kingpost truss	iron	tramway to carry limestone and water for ironworks	63
pontoon	wooden barges, steel cables	sank 1809, killing thousands	130
woven organic	fig tree roots	Ficus elastica. Described 1844, probably much older	25
box girder	wrought iron	tubular design, first box girders, extensive modeling	59
three-story arch	brick	largest brick bridge in the world; early use of structural analysis	44
segmental arch	cast iron	2nd cast iron bridge in America, looks light	58
cantilever, segmental arch	steel	Innovations include steel, caissons, and cantilever method	68
lattice truss	steel	collapsed in wind, Dec. 1879	130
suspension	steel	largest suspension bridge when built; Gothic towers were the largest structures in the Americas	74
cantilever arch	steel	built in seven months for Cornelius Vanderbilt	91
swinging pontoon	boats, wood	operator opens the bridge with diesel powered propeller	86
cantilever	steel	spans of 520 m were longest cantilever spans at the time	92
bascule and suspension	steel and stone	steam power originally lifted the bascules, now electric power	87
segmental arch	concrete	Maillart style, open spandrel, destroyed by avalanche in 1927	103
reticular truss over parabolic arch	concrete and steel	planned by Cecil Rhodes; now has bungee jumping	108

Bridge Name	Year completed	Country	Barrier crossed	Overall length
Quebec Bridge	1907	Canada, Quebec	St. Lawrence R.	2600 m
Veurdre Bridge	1910	France	Allier R.	218 m
Chengyang Bridge	1912	China	Linxi R.	64 m
Winkley Bridge	1912	USA, Arkansas	Little Red R.	168 m
Silver Bridge	1928	USA, Ohio-West Virginia	Ohio R.	681 m
Salginatobel Bridge	1930	Switzerland	Schiers Valley	133 m
Sydney Harbor Bridge	1932	Australia	Sydney Harbor	504 m span
Cape Cod Canal Railway Bridge	1935	USA, Massachusetts	Cape Cod Canal	166 m span
San Francisco-Oakland Bay Bridge	1936	USA, California	S. Francisco Bay	7180 m
Golden Gate Bridge	1937	USA, California	mouth of S. Francisco Bay	1970 m
Qiantang River Bridge	1937	China, Hangzhou	Qiantang R.	1453 m
Tacoma Narrows Bridge	1940	USA, Washington	strait of Puget Sound	1646 m
Howrah Bridge	1942	India, Calcutta	Hooghly R.	705 m
Kampong Cham Bamboo Bridge	1940s or before	Cambodia	Mekong R.	1000 m
Sunshine Skyway Bridge	1954	USA, Florida	Lower Tampa Bay	6.7 km

Style	Material used	Comments	Page
cantilever	steel	collapsed during construction—twice	132
three span arch	concrete	Frysinnet used models and reinforced concrete	104
covered corridor and pavilions	wood	no nails or rivets, built by Dong people, "Wind and Rain" bridge	50
suspension	wood and steel	"swinging bridge" collapsed 1996, killing five	143
suspension	steel	eyebar chain gave out in Dec 1967; collapse with 46 deaths	138
segmental arch with hollow box girder	reinforced concrete	light and airy, Maillart style	104
through arch	steel, concrete and granite	called "the iron lung" and "the coathanger;" use of creeper cranes	109
vertical lift	steel	built during Depression over man-made canal	88
cantilever truss	steel and concrete	during 1989 earthquake, section of upper deck collapsed onto lower deck, killing one	140
suspension	galvanized steel	red-orange color shows up well in fog; first use of hardhats and safety netting	94
two-tier truss	steel	blown up after only 89 days in anti-Japanese war	66
suspension	steel	"Galloping Gertie," classic resonant collapse four months after opening	134
cantilever	steel	heaviest traffic of any bridge in Asia	93
trestle	bamboo	constructed and taken down by locals each year	20
truss	concrete	struck by freighter during 1980 storm; 35 people died in bridge collapse	141

Bridge Name	Year completed	Country	Barrier crossed	Overall length
Lake Pontchartrain Causeway	1957	USA, Louisiana	Lake Pontchartrain	38.4 km
Rio-Niterói	1974	Brazil	Guanabara Bay	13.3 km
West Gate Bridge	1978	Australia	Yarra R.	2.58 km
Corinth Canal Bridge	1988	Greece	Corinth Canal	16 m?
Bergsøysund	1992	Norway	Bergsøysundet Strait	931 m
Alamillo Bridge	1992	Spain	Guadalquivir	250 m
Akashi Kaikyo	1998	Japan	Akashi Strait	3911 m
London Millennium Footbridge	2000	England, London	Thames R.	325 m
Gateshead Millennium Bridge	2001	England, Newcastle	Tyne R.	126 m
Juscelino Kubitschek Bridge	2002	Brazil	Lake Paranoá	1200 m
Zakim Bridge	2003	USA, Massachusetts	Charles R.	436 m
Millau Viaduct	2004	France	Tarn Valley	2460 m
Penobscot Narrows	2006	USA, Maine	Penobscot R.	646 m
Hangzhou Bay Bridge	2008	China, Zhejiang	Hangzhou Bay	36 km
Samuel Beckett Bridge	2009	Ireland	Liffey R.	120 m

Style	Material used	Comments	Page
beam/girder	concrete	longest continuous bridge over water	121
girder	pre-stressed concrete	longest girder bridge in southern hemisphere	82
cable-stayed box girder	steel	collapse during construction in 1970 killed 35	83
submersible	steel	narrow canal, small ships pass above	89
pontoon	concrete and steel	Seven concrete pontoons rise and fall four meters in the tide	105
cable-stayed	steel	built for Expo '92	115
suspension	steel	slightly longer after earthquake	99
suspension	steel	very low profile; initial problem with swaying solved by dampers	148
rotating cable-stayed arch	steel	movable bridge, called "the blinking eye"	150
arch	steel	asymmetric; arches cross the bridge diagonally	111
cable-stayed	concrete and steel	widest cable-stayed bridge, ten lanes	118
cable-stayed	concrete and steel	taller than Eiffel Tower	116
cable-stayed	concrete and steel	cradle system for stays; observatory in one tower	119
cable-stayed and box girder	concrete and steel	longest continuous bridge over ocean, GPS used to position pilings	123
cable-stayed	concrete and steel	looks like an Irish harp	115

Bridge Name	Year completed	Country	Barrier crossed	Overall length
Kurilpa Footbridge	2009	Australia, Queensland	Brisbane R.	470 m
Sheikh Zayed Bridge	2010	UAE, Abu Dhabi	bay	831 m
Moses Bridge	2010	Netherlands	Fort de Roovere moat	10 m?
crab bridges	2015	Easter Island	highways	short
Danyang-Kunshan Grand Bridge	2011	China, Shanghai-Nanjing	Yangtze R. delta	164.8 km
Zhangjiajie Glass Bridge	2016	China, Hunan	forest canyon	430 m
Hong Kong-Zhuhai-Macao Bridge	2018	China	Pearl R. delta	54.7 km

Style	Material used	Comments	Page
tensegrity	steel	twenty steel masts look like knitting needles	155
arch	steel	undulating wave-like arches, road passes through	112
trench	wood	pedestrians walk below water level	153
truss?	steel mesh	>30 underpasses also; 50 million crabs	161
girders	concrete	longest land bridge, trains travel at up to 300 kph	125
suspension	steel and glass	pedestrians can look down through transparent deck 300 meters to forest floor	151
beam, trestle, undersea tunnel	concrete and steel	$20 billion to build; longest (discontinuous) bridge over water	126

Glossary

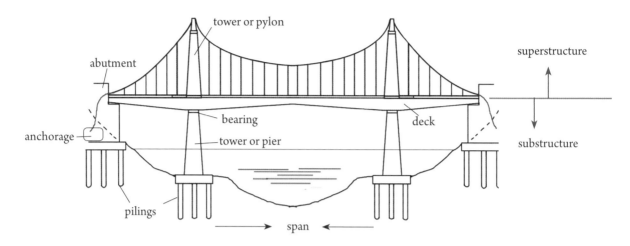

Abutment – The structure at each end of a bridge that supports the ends and resists the outward pressing forces of, for example, an arch bridge. It is often built of stone or concrete. The abutment transfers forces from the bridge to the soil. See above.

Aerial roots – Roots of a tree that start partway up the trunk and arch downward. These are common in fig trees and can be used to weave a bridge.

Alloy – A substance made of two mixed metals (e.g. bronze or brass), or of metal mixed with non-metal (e.g. stainless steel)

Anchorage – A structure at either end of a suspension bridge that pins down and holds the ends of suspension cables. The anchorage may be in the bridge abutment, farther ashore, or even underground.

Aqueduct – A structure that carries water from one place to another, usually elevated, traditionally built of stone.

Arch – A curved structure spanning a gap or opening. Traditionally built of stone, it can also use concrete, iron, or steel. The form of the arch causes its elements to be primarily in compression under any load.

Bowstring arch (also often called a "tied arch") – All arches push outward at their bottom ends. The two bottom ends of a bowstring arch are attached by a beam or connector that counteracts the outward force, just as a bowstring holds a bow in its bent position. The connector is primarily in tension.

Corbel arch – An arch-like structure where layers of stone project farther and farther into a gap, without mortar.

Gothic arch – An arch with a sharply pointed top, common in Gothic cathedrals, also seen in the arches of the Brooklyn Bridge's towers.

True arch or **voussoir arch** – An arch consisting of carefully cut stones, narrower at one end than another. Mortar may be used between the stones. These wedge-like stones allow construction of a half circle in which all elements are in compression, and the downward force is transferred outward and down along the arch to the ground.

Safavid arch – An arch with a shallow, pointed top, characteristic of Persian architecture.

segmental or **segmented arch** – A partial arch, not a full semi-circle.

Bascule – A drawbridge whose pivoting section is raised and lowered using counterweights.

The bridge on the cover of this book is a bascule bridge.

Beam bridge – The simplest kind of bridge, with a straight beam crossing a gap. Because this kind of bridge is not particularly strong, a single beam cannot cross a wide gap.

beam bridge bending under weight

Bending – Distortion of a straight component without twisting.

Bridge – A structure that spans a gap, allowing people, animals, vehicles or water to cross.

Bridge bearings– Supports allowing the superstructure to rest upon the abutment and piers.

Bridge bearings are generally roller, pinned, or fixed.

A roller support transfers vertical loads but allows the structures to move horizontally relative to each other and allows rotation.

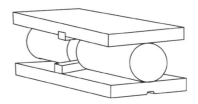

A pinned support transfers vertical and horizontal forces but allows rotation.

A spherical bearing allows the bridge to rock in any direction.

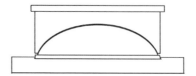

A fixed support does not allow translation or rotation but may cushion against vibration as in an elastomeric bearing.

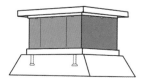

Bungee jumping – Jumping from a high, fixed object while attached to an elastic cord (the bungee), usually by the feet. The jumper bounces up and down before coming to a rest and being helped down from the final hanging position.

Cable-stayed bridge – A bridge in which the load is supported by cables running diagonally from the bridge deck to one or more towers or pylons.

Cantilever – A structure projecting out into empty space from one fixed end. A diving board is a familiar example. Cantilever construction can be used when an engineer does not want to build scaffolding structures up from below. From piers, this is only possible if the cantilever extends from both sides of the pier so they counterbalance each other. A cantilever bridge will often have two cantilevers that join in the middle.

Caisson – A large chamber, watertight but open at the bottom, which is filled with compressed air and lowered into a body of water to allow construction work at the water's bottom. (See page 72.)

Caisson disease – The "bends" or compression sickness; the effect of nitrogen gas that has been dissolved in blood bubbling out and blocking blood flow as a person comes out of a high-pressure space, like a caisson, into lower pressure, like the surface.

Catenary – The curve a hanging chain or cable makes naturally when supporting only its own weight. When the cable has to support a weight much larger than itself, like the deck of a bridge, the curve will come closer to the shape of a parabola.

Cement – A soft material, usually of clay or lime, that when mixed with water dries hard and stone-like, and can be mixed with stones and sand to make concrete. Hydraulic cement can harden even underwater.

Cistern – A holding tank for water that allows silt to settle out at the bottom.

Cofferdam – A watertight structure set in water, which is then pumped dry to allow work inside it, below the waterline. Cofferdams have been used since Roman times in the construction of bridge piers.

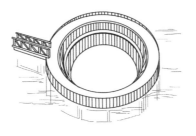

Compression – A force that tends to push something together or crush it.

Concrete – A building material made of cement, gravel, sand, and water, that hardens upon drying. Concrete is strong in compression, but very weak in tension.

Reinforced concrete – Concrete that includes a material that is good at resisting tension, usually steel bars.

Constraints – Limitations or conditions that a design must satisfy. For example, a bridge might need to be at least a certain height, cost no more than a certain amount, and be safe in an earthquake that measures 7.0 on the Richter scale.

Corrosion – The gradual chemical destruction of a metal through natural forces. An example is rusting.

Counterweight – A weight that exerts force in the opposite direction from lifting, making lifting easier and more efficient. Counterweights are used in cranes, in cantilever construction and in bascule bridges, for example.

Covered bridge – A bridge with a roof to protect it from the elements. Covered wooden bridges were common in early America.

Deck – A bridge's roadway or surface that allows traffic and pedestrians to cross. It us usually made of wood, steel, concrete, or grating, often covered with a crossing surface such as asphalt for cars, or rails for trains.

Dovetail - A mortise and tenon joint.

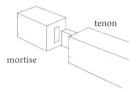

Ductile – Bendable, not brittle. A ductile metal can be pulled out into a thin wire.

Eyebar – A metal bar enlarged and flattened at each end to allow for a hole. An eyebar is used as a connector under tension in bridges and trusses.

Falsework – The scaffolding built underneath to support a bridge while it is under construction.

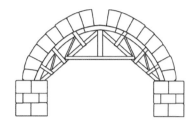

Foundation – The part of the structure that transfers forces to the soil or rock below.

Glubam – A building material of thin layers of bamboo glued together.

Glulam - A building material of thin layers of wood glued together.

Girder – The main support beam of a bridge. It is horizontal and supports smaller crossbeams. Usually made of concrete, iron or steel.

Box girder – A hollow iron or steel girder with a square or rectangular cross-section, for maximum strength for its weight.

I-beam – A beam, usually of steel, that looks like a capital I in cross-section. The horizontal parts of the beam are called the flanges, and the center vertical part is called the web. Laid on its side, an I-beam becomes an H-beam. Without the bottom flange, an I-beam becomes a T-beam.

Iron – A metal, element number 26, with chemical symbol Fe. By weight the most common element in the Earth, it has been used since ancient times. The Iron Age began as early as 1200 BCE in the Middle East and South Asia.

Cast iron – Iron that has been melted and poured into a mold to cool. Cast iron has a relatively low melting point (1150 to 1200 °C) and was first used in ancient times when people began heating iron ore. It usually contains 2-4% carbon. Although it has high compressive strength, meaning it can't easily be crushed, it has low tensile strength, meaning it can be stretched. Cast iron also tends to be brittle and crack easily.

Wrought iron – Iron alloy with less than 0.08% carbon, that has been heated and then worked with tools. (Think of the village blacksmith.) The more it is worked, the stronger it gets. It is tough and when hot can be beaten or shaped into different forms. Wrought iron tends to have a grain like wood. Compared to cast iron, wrought iron has high tensile strength and relatively low compressive strength. However, it is brittle compared to steel, which today has almost totally replaced it.

Load – The forces that a bridge must resist, including the weight of the bridge and passing traffic, wind loads, and earthquake loads.

Dead load – The weight of the bridge structure, railings, deck, etc., when nothing is crossing it.

Live load – The weight of whatever crosses the bridge: people, cars and trucks, trains, and more.

Masonry – Stonework or brickwork.

Mortar – A mixture of lime or cement with sand or water, used to bind stones or bricks together.

Mortise and tenon – A kind of joint used in carpentry. A projecting piece of wood or tongue of the tenon fits snugly into a hole in the mortise. Mortise and tenon construction is thousands of years old.

Pier – A tower set in water to support a bridge. See top of page 188.

Pile (plural is pilings) – A structure driven into the soil to provide the foundation of a bridge. Pilings may extend from the bottom of a pier. See top of page 188.

Pontoon bridge – A floating bridge built across a series of anchored boats or chambers.

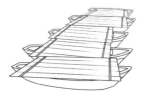

Portico – An open structure with a roof supported by columns. A portico is usually a porch for a larger building.

Pylon – A support tower or structure used for a suspension bridge or highway, often built of steel. See top of page 188.

Rebar – Short for "reinforcing bar." Rebar is a steel bar or mesh used to reinforce concrete and other building materials.

Shear – A kind of stress or force that pushes in a direction that is not axial. That is, it is not pushing along the main axis of a component. An example might be a river pushing on the piers of a bridge, or wind pushing against the superstructure.

Span – The part of a bridge or length of the bridge deck between supports. See top of page 188.

Spandrel – The triangular space between the outer curve of an arch and the side and ceiling of the structure it is supporting. Spandrels may be open or closed.

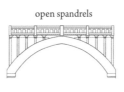
open spandrels

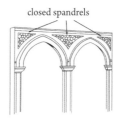
closed spandrels

Steel – An alloy of iron, about 2% carbon, and a variety of other materials, such as silicon, chromium, or magnesium. Steel is harder and stronger than iron, combining the compressive strength of cast iron with the tensile strength of wrought iron. Steel is more ductile than iron: it is not brittle and can change shape without losing strength.

> **Galvanized steel** – Steel that has been coated with zinc to prevent corrosion.

> **Stainless steel** – A steel alloy with more than 10% chromium that resists corrosion.

> **Weathering steel** – An alloy of steel where the surface rusts in a way that creates a resistant covering preventing further corrosion without painting.

Substructure – Everything below the bridge roadway. The substructure supports the superstructure. It transfers the load from the superstructure to the soil or rock below. Piers and abutments are part of the substructure.

Structural analysis – A method for figuring out all the loads and forces affecting the different parts of a structure.

Superstructure – A structure built atop something else. Many trusses are superstructures, built above a bridge roadway. The part of the bridge structure that is above (or supported by) the piers and abutments is the superstructure.

Suspension bridge – A type of bridge in which the bridge deck is hung from suspension cables that are strung across a gap over towers. Vertical cables hang from the suspension cables to support the bridge deck.

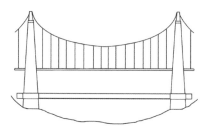

Swing bridge – A movable bridge in which one section swivels ninety degrees to open one or more channels, allowing water traffic to pass.

Tension – A force that tends to pull materials apart, the opposite of compression.

Torsion – Twisting about an axis that runs the length of any bridge component.

Trestle – A framework with a horizontal crossbar supported by two pairs of sloping legs, like a sawhorse. In a trestle bridge, the roadway can be built across these horizontal crossbars. Many wooden railroad bridges were trestle bridges, usually meant to be temporary.

Truss bridge – Bridge that features a support structure made up of straight components arranged in rigid triangles, either above or below the deck. The components resist both compression and tension. Early truss bridges were built of wood, but today they are generally made of steel, or sometimes reinforced concrete. See page 64 for some examples.

Vertical lift bridge – A movable bridge in which a section of the span rises straight up to allow water traffic to pass below.

Windlass – A turning device for hauling or lifting something. It's usually a cylinder turned by a crank or by handles. Rope is pulled around the cylinder, which rotates as the windlass turns. A person cranking a handle to lift a bucket of water out of a well is using a windlass.

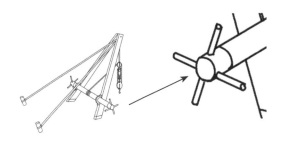

Further Reading

Once you start loving bridges, you'll want to see more of them. Here are a few books you may want to explore. Some have beautiful photographs, others fascinating stories.

Adkins, Jan. *Bridges: From My Side to Yours.* Roaring Book Press, Brookfield CT, 2002. Black and white drawings illustrate the history of bridges and how they are built.

Agrawal, Roma. *Built: The Hidden Stories Behind Our Structures.* Bloomsbury USA, 2018. Not just about bridges, this is a readable, award-winning book about structural engineering (a branch of civil engineering) by the woman behind Western Europe's tallest building.

Brown, David J. *Bridges: Three Thousand Years of Defying Nature.* MBI Publishing, St. Paul, MN, 2001. This book addresses the history, physics, and construction of bridges. It includes both photographs and explanatory drawings. The text is mostly captions.

Dupre, Judith. *Bridges: A History of the World's Most Spectacular Spans.* Black Dog and Leventhal Publishers, New York, 2017. This book has an unusual, long, horizontal design, and it contains interviews with various bridge designers.

Farrow, August. *Bridgescapes: A Photographic Collection of Scenic Bridges.* Seamonkey Ink, 2017. Available as a Kindle edition, this book features beautiful photographs of bridges of all sorts.

MacDonald, Donald and Ira Nadel, *Golden Gate Bridge.* Chronicle Books, San Francisco, 2008. The authors look especially at the art and design of the bridge, with helpful drawings.

McCullough, David. *The Great Bridge: The Epic Story of the Building of the Brooklyn Bridge.* Simon & Schuster, New York, 1972. This readable, in-depth biography of a bridge is still in print. It formed the basis for a 1981 documentary by Ken Burns.

Miller, Howard and Quinta Scott. *The Eads Bridge*, Missouri History Museum Press, 1999. This photographic essay, originally published in 1979, considers the bridge as art and architecture as well as providing an insight into the age of railway barons.

Perino, Angia Sassi, and Giorgio Faraggiana. *Bridges: Triumphs of Engineering*. Barnes and Noble Books, New York, 2004. Arranged more or less historically, and translated from Italian, this book contains stunning photographs of 35 bridges.

Nardo, Don. *Roman Roads and Aqueducts*, Lucent Books, 2000. As it describes and illustrates building technology and design evolved during Roman times, this book also presents interesting information on lives, people, and customs of ancient Rome.

Plowden, David. *Bridges: The Spans of North America*. Norton, NY, 2002. As the title indicates, this book focuses on North America, with 187 beautiful black-and-white photographs, along with stories of who built them and how.

Stearns, Cyrus. *King of the Empty Plain: The Tibetan Iron-Bridge Builder Tangtong Gyalpo*. Snow Lion, 2007. This is an account of traditional and historical knowledge about the Tibetan monk, well known in the Himalayan region but little known in the West.

Watson, Bruce. *Old London Bridge Lost and Found*. Museum of London Archeology, 2004. Part of the popular Lost and Found series, this book, which has more illustrations than text, shows how one bridge evolved from Roman times to the present.

Photo and Image Credits

JEG7340.jpg by PJeganathan [CC BY-SA 4.0 (https://creativecommons.org/licenses/by-sa/4.0)] (edited)

p.22 Mawlynnong's Living Root Bridge in Meghalaya, India, https://commons.wikimedia.org/wiki/File:Mawlynnong%27s_Living_Root_Bridge_in_Meghalaya,_India.jpg Sujan Bandyopadhyay [CC BY-SA 4.0 (https://creativecommons.org/licenses/by-sa/4.0)]

p.23 top The Stone Arch Bridge across the Mississippi River in Minneapolis, MN by Paul VanDerWerf

Chapter 4

p.23 bottom https://commons.wikimedia.org/wiki/File:Annibale_Carracci,_The_Cyclops_Polyphemus.jpg Annibale Carracci [Public domain]

p.24 top https://commons.wikimedia.org/wiki/File:Arkadiko_Mycenaean_Bridge_II.JPG Flausa123 [CC BY-SA 3.0 (https://creativecommons.org/licenses/by-sa/3.0)]

p.24 https://commons.wikimedia.org/wiki/File:Corbel_Arch.svg, Ricraider [CC BY-SA 3.0 (https://creativecommons.org/licenses/by-sa/3.0)] https://commons.wikimedia.org/wiki/File:Arc_truefalserp.jpg, No machine-readable author provided. Anton~commonswiki assumed (based on copyright claims). [CC BY-SA 2.5 (https://creativecommons.org/licenses/by-sa/2.5)]

p.25 Alcantara bridge, https://commons.wikimedia.org/wiki/File:The_Alc%C3%A1ntara_Bridge_built_over_the_Tagus_River_between_104_and_106_AD_by_a_man_named_Caius_Julius_Lacer,_and_dedicated_to_the_Roman_emperor_Trajan,_Spain_(26704597218).jpg

Carole Raddato from FRANKFURT, Germany [CC BY-SA 2.0 (https://creativecommons.org/licenses/by-sa/2.0)]

p.26 Cofferdam, https://commons.wikimedia.org/wiki/File:Cofferdam_Olmsted_Locks_Ohio_River.jpg U.S. Army Corps of Engineers, photographer not specified or unknown [Public domain]

Bridge pier, https://commons.wikimedia.org/wiki/File:Bridge_Piers_P2110004_US_27_Central_Ave.JPG Chris Light [CC BY-SA 4.0 (https://creativecommons.org/licenses/by-sa/4.0)]

p.27 Segovia Aqueduct, https://commons.wikimedia.org/wiki/File:Aqueduct_of_Segovia_1824_Edward_Hawke_Locker.jpg Edward Hawke Locker (1777-1849) [Public domain]

p.28 https://pxhere.com/en/photo/1215666 (public domain)

p.29 Pont du Gard, https://commons.wikimedia.org/w/index.php?curid=33474941, by Benh LIEU SONG - Own work, CC BY-SA 3.0

p.29 bottom line drawing by Chen-Hui Chang

p.30 Le Pont du Garde, France by Mike McBey, https://www.flickr.com/photos/158652122@N02/39894623680 CC BY 2.0

Chapter 5

p.31 https://commons.wikimedia.org/wiki/File:Interstate_90_floating_bridges_after_Blue_Angels_performance_-_01.jpg, SounderBruce [CC BY-SA 4.0 (https://creativecommons.org/licenses/by-sa/4.0)]

p.32 map https://upload.wikimedia.org/wikipedia/commons/a/a5/Dardanelles_map2.png by ChrisO, public domain

p.32 https://commons.wikimedia.org/wiki/File:Xerxes_crossing_the_Hellespont.jpg, Edmund OllierPublication date 1882 [Public domain]

p.33 Donjin floating bridge in the 1940s, https://commons.wikimedia.org/wiki/File:Gannan_1940s.jpg, public domain

p.34 top Roman pontoon bridge, Column of Marcus Aurelius, Rome https://commons.wikimedia.org/wiki/File:Roman_Pontoon_Bridge,_Column_of_Marcus_Aurelius,_Rome,_Italy.jpg, User:MatthiasKabel [CC BY-SA 3.0 (https://creativecommons.org/licenses/by-sa/3.0)]

p.34 bottom, background https://commons.wikimedia.org/wiki/File:1561-Akbar_riding_the_elephant_Hawa%27I_pursuing_another_elephant_across_a_collapsing_bridge_of_boats_(left).jpg, Victoria and Albert Museum [Public domain]

p.35 https://commons.wikimedia.org/wiki/File:US_Army_crossing_the_Rhine_on_heavy_ponton_bridge_at_Worms,_March,_1945.png public domain

Chapter 6

p.36 https://commons.wikimedia.org/wiki/File:Zhaozhou_Bridge.jpg, Zhao 1974 [Public domain]

p.37 line drawing, Chen-Hui Chang

p.38 top Cosimo I de' Medici in armour by Agnolo Bronzino (public domain) pp.38 39 Panorama of the Ponte Vecchio in Florence, Italy (seen from the West), https://upload.wikimedia.org/wikipedia/commons/7/77/Panorama_of_the_Ponte_Vecchio_in_Florence%2C_Italy.jpg, Jan Drewes [CC BY-SA 4.0 (https://creativecommons.org/licenses/by-sa/4.0)]

p.40 Realto, Rialto Bridge at night. Venice, Italy by Livioandronico2013, https://commons.wikimedia.org/wiki/File:Rialto_Bridge_at_night2.jpg. Livioandronico2013 [CC BY-SA 4.0 (https://creativecommons.org/licenses/by-sa/4.0)]

p.42 top https://fr.wikipedia.org/wiki/Fichier:Masjed-e_Shah_0.JPG#file. Shah Mosque Isfahan by Self, GFDL

p.42 bottom https://www.flickr.com/photos/super_lapin/10653374693 by Richard Weil, Attribution-NoDerivs 2.0 Generic (CC BY-ND 2.0)

p.43 top https://commons.wikimedia.org/wiki/File:Si-o-seh_pol,_Esfahan,_Iran.jpg, Hamidreza Bagheri [CC BY-SA 4.0 (https://creativecommons.org/licenses/by-sa/4.0)]

p.43 bottom https://commons.wikimedia.org/wiki/File:Si-o-se_Pol,_Isfah%C3%A1n,_Ir%C3%A1n,_2016-09-20,_DD_91.jpg, Diego Delso [CC BY-SA 4.0 (https://creativecommons.org/licenses/by-sa/4.0)]

Chapter 7

p.44 Göltzsch Viaduct 1851, https://commons.wikimedia.org/wiki/File:G%C3%B6ltzschtalbr%C3%BCcke_2012.jpg Göltzschtalbrücke 2012 by user:UlrichAAB [CC BY 3.0 (https://creativecommons.org/licenses/by/3.0)]

p.45 https://commons.wikimedia.org/wiki/File:Auf_der_G%C3%B6ltzschtalbr%C3%BCcke..._IMG_0067OB.jpg by Kora27 [CC BY-SA 4.0 (https://creativecommons.org/licenses/by-sa/4.0)]

Chapter 8

pp.46 47 https://de.wikipedia.org/wiki/Datei:Luzern_Kapellbr%C3%BCcke_1180623.jpg by Reinhold Möller, Attribution 4.0 International (CC BY 4.0)

p.48 https://commons.wikimedia.org/wiki/File:Kapellbr%C3%BCcke_Tafel_49.JPG, James Steakley [CC BY-SA 4.0 (https://creativecommons.org/licenses/by-sa/4.0)]

p.49 https://commons.wikimedia.org/wiki/File:Bridge_in_Cambridge.JPG. Dbauer271 [CC BY-SA 3.0 (https://creativecommons.org/licenses/by-sa/3.0)]

p.49 https://commons.wikimedia.org/wiki/File:Mathematical_Bridge_tangents.jpg. Cmglee [CC BY-SA 3.0 (https://creativecommons.org/licenses/by-sa/3.0)]

p.50 https://commons.wikimedia.org/wiki/File:Sanjiang_Chengyang_Yongji_Qiao_2012.10.02_17-44-29.jpg, Zhangzhugang [CC BY-SA 3.0 (https://creativecommons.org/licenses/by-sa/3.0)]

p.51 https://commons.wikimedia.org/wiki/File:Sanjiang_Chengyang_Yongji_Qiao_2012.10.02_17-51-22.jpg Sanjiang Chengyang Yongji Qiao by Zhangzhugang

p.51 line drawing by Chen-Hui Chang

p.52 top Sanjiang Chengyang Yongji Qiao 2012.10.02 17-40-17. https://commons.wikimedia.org/wiki/File:Sanjiang_Chengyang_Yongji_Qiao_2012.10.02_17-40-17.jpg Zhangzhugang [CC BY-SA 3.0 (https://creativecommons.org/licenses/by-sa/3.0)]

p.52 bottom left Guo Moruo, https://commons.wikimedia.org/wiki/File:Guo_Moruo_1942.JPG, National Museum of China [Public domain]

p.52 bottom right https://en.wikipedia.org/wiki/File:Sanjiang_Chengyang_Yongji_Qiao_2012.10.02_17-39-10.jpg Sanjiang Chengyang Yongji Qiao 2012.10.02 17-39-10, Zhangzhugang, GFDL

Chapter 9

p.53 top https://commons.wikimedia.org/wiki/File:The_Iron_Bridge_(8542).jpg. Nilfanion [CC BY-SA 4.0 (https://creativecommons.org/licenses/by-sa/4.0)]

p.53 bottom https://en.wikipedia.org/wiki/Thang_Tong_Gyalpo#/media/File:TangtonGyalpo.jpg, public domain

p.54 https://en.wikipedia.org/wiki/File:Old_Chain-Bridge_at_Chaksam.jpg public domain.

p.55 https://en.wikipedia.org/wiki/Chakzam_Bridge#/media/File:Chaksam_(Iron_Bridge_in_transliteration_from_Tibetan_to_English).png, public domain

p.56 https://commons.wikimedia.org/wiki/File:Tamchog_Chakzam,_Bhutan_09.jpg. Bernard Gagnon [CC BY-SA 4.0 (https://creativecommons.org/licenses/by-sa/4.0)] (cropped)

p.57 Iron Bridge and close-up: https://www.flickr.com/photos/mdpettitt/37327827462 , Martin Pettitt, Attribution 2.0 Generic (CC BY 2.0)

p.58 Bow bridge, https://upload.wikimedia.org/wikipedia/commons/d/d9/Bow_Bridge_in_Central_Park_on_

Chapter 13

p.79 https://commons.wikimedia.org/wiki/File:Girder_Bridge_(31037203990).jpg. Tony Hisgett from Birmingham, UK [CC BY 2.0 (https://creativecommons.org/licenses/by/2.0)]

pp. 80 81 line drawing by Chen-Hui Chang

p.82 https://upload.wikimedia.org/wikipedia/commons/4/43/Rio-Niter%C3%B3i_Bridge_DSC_7410_%2816586021942%29.jpg. Juliana Swenson from Phoenix, U.S.A. [CC BY-SA 2.0 (https://creativecommons.org/licenses/by-sa/2.0)]

p.83 https://www.oldtreasurybuilding.org.au/past-exhibitions/westgate-bridge-collapse-40-years-on/ VPRS 24/P3 Inquest Deposition Files, unit 120, by permission of the Public Records Office Victoria, Australia

p.84 https://upload.wikimedia.org/wikipedia/commons/f/f6/West-Gate-Bridge-Melbourne-2008.jpg Kham Tran - www.khamtran.com [CC BY-SA 3.0 (https://creativecommons.org/licenses/by-sa/3.0)]

Chapter 14

p.85 https://commons.wikimedia.org/wiki/File:Cape_Cod_Bourne_Bridge_and_Railroad_Bridge.jpg U.S. Army Corps of Engineers, photographer not specified or unknown [Public domain]

pp. 86, 87 https://upload.wikimedia.org/wikipedia/commons/2/20/Closing_of_the_Queen_Emma_Pontoon_Bridge%2C_Willemstad_%284386304187%29.jpg. Charles Hoffman from New York, United States [CC BY-SA 2.0 (https://creativecommons.org/licenses/by-sa/2.0)]

p.87 https://upload.wikimedia.org/wikipedia/commons/thumb/5/51/Tower_Bridge_London_June_2016_002.jpg/4096px-Tower_Bridge_London_June_2016_002.jpg. King of Hearts [CC BY-SA 4.0 (https://creativecommons.org/licenses/by-sa/4.0)]

p.88 https://commons.wikimedia.org/wiki/File:USA_Massachusetts_location_map.svg, Alexrk2 [CC BY 3.0 (https://creativecommons.org/licenses/by/3.0)]

p.89 https://upload.wikimedia.org/wikipedia/commons/f/fb/BridgeSubmerging4.jpg. Aspasia Coumiotis [CC BY-SA 1.0 (https://creativecommons.org/licenses/by-sa/1.0)]

Chapter 15

p.90 https://commons.wikimedia.org/wiki/File:Forth_Bridge_(15095755025).jpg. andrum99 [CC BY-SA 2.0 (https://creativecommons.org/licenses/by-sa/2.0)]

p.91 top https://commons.wikimedia.org/wiki/File:Cantilever_bridge_human_model.jpg. Unknown photographer for Benjamin Baker. [Public domain]

p.91 bottom https://en.wikipedia.org/wiki/Whirlpool_Rapids_Bridge#/media/File:Niagara_Falls_Suspension_Bridge_to_Lower_Steel_Arch_Bridge_3.jpg, [Public domain] Buck, Richard (December 1898). "The Niagara Railway Arch"

p.92 https://commons.wikimedia.org/wiki/File:William_Morris_age_53.jpg. Frederick Hollyer [Public domain]

p.93 https://commons.wikimedia.org/wiki/File:River_Hooghly_%26_Howrah_Bridge_-_Ram_Chandra_Goenka_Zenana_Bathing_Ghat_-_Kolkata_2012-10-15_0782.JPG (cropped), Biswarup Ganguly [CC BY 3.0 (https://creativecommons.org/licenses/by/3.0)]

Chapter 16

p.94 https://en.wikipedia.org/wiki/File:GoldenGateBridge-001.jpg#file by Rich Niewiroski Jr., source: http://www.projectrich.com/gallery, Attribution 2.5 Generic (CC BY 2.5)

pp.96 97 https://www.pexels.com/photo/blue-bridge-golden-gate-bridge-ocean-2284171/ Photo by Maarten van den Heuvel from Pexels

pp.100 101 https://upload.wikimedia.org/wikipedia/commons/1/12/Akashi_Kaikyo_Ohashi_01.jpg. Pinqui [Public domain]

Chapter 17

p.102 top https://upload.wikimedia.org/wikipedia/commons/b/bc/Pont_b%C3%A9ton_-_Jardin_des_Plantes_%28Grenoble%29.jpg. Matthieu Riegler, CC-by [CC BY 3.0 (https://creativecommons.org/licenses/by/3.0)]

p.102 bottom https://upload.wikimedia.org/wikipedia/commons/2/27/2085f_Japon_Hatoma.jpg Psammophile [CC BY-SA 3.0 (https://creativecommons.org/licenses/by-sa/3.0)]

p.103 top https://upload.wikimedia.org/wikipedia/commons/thumb/1/19/ETH-BIB-Maillart%2C_Robert_%281872-1940%29-Portrait-Portr_13004.tif/lossy-page1-2952px-ETH-BIB-Maillart%2C_Robert_%281872-1940%29-Portrait-Portr_13004.tif.jpg, ETH Library [Public domain]

p.126 https://stock.adobe.com/images/beijing-shanghai-high-speed-railway-passes-through-rivers-and-lakes/168685474

p.127 https://de.wikipedia.org/wiki/Datei:HZMB_route.svg#file, source Own Work, Kellykaneshiro , Reference: THe HZMB website http://www.hzmb.hk/ Note: As for the Hong kong area, Hong Kong Tuen Mun District.svg, 19:38, 21 Aug 2015 OgreBot2 version, Attribution-ShareAlike 4.0 international.(modified to simplified Chinese, removed HKSR boundary line)

p.128 https://upload.wikimedia.org/wikipedia/commons/5/55/Pink_Dolphin.JPG, user:takoradee, DFDL

Chapter 21

pp.128 129 background https://upload.wikimedia.org/wikipedia/commons/a/ab/Ponte_das_Barcas%2C_desenho_do_Bar%C3%A3o_de_Forrester.jpeg. by Joseph James Forrester, public domain

p.130 https://commons.wikimedia.org/wiki/File:A_Cat%C3%A1strofe_da_Ponte_das_Barcas_(1809).png public domain

p.131 top https://upload.wikimedia.org/wikipedia/commons/c/c3/Original_Tay_Bridge_before_the_1879_collapse.jpg public domain

p.131 bottom https://en.wikipedia.org/wiki/File:Catastrophe_du_pont_sur_le_Tay_-_1879_-_Illustration.jpg public domain

p.132 https://commons.wikimedia.org/wiki/File:William_McGonagall.jpg, Parisian Photo Co, Edinburgh [Public domain]

p.133 top https://upload.wikimedia.org/wikipedia/commons/2/2d/Pont_de_Quebec_1907.jpg. Neurdein [Public domain]

p.133 bottom https://commons.wikimedia.org/wiki/File:Floating_centre_span_downstream,_Quebec_Bridge,_Quebec_City,_QC,_1916.jpg public domain

p.134 https://upload.wikimedia.org/wikipedia/commons/e/e4/Tacoma_Narrows_Bridge_opening_program_June_30%2C_1940.jpg Tacoma Narrows Bridge - McChord Field Celebration Committee, Norton Clapp, General Chairman; Prepared by Shannon Brothers; Published by Johnson-Cox Company, Tacoma, WA [Public domain]

p.135 https://upload.wikimedia.org/wikipedia/commons/e/ec/Mount_Rainier_at_the_Tacoma_Narrows_Bridge_%2818402622459%29.jpg. Jonathan Miske from United States [CC BY-SA 2.0 (https://creativecommons.org/licenses/by-sa/2.0)]i

p.137 https://upload.wikimedia.org/wikipedia/commons/e/e5/Crater_Lake%2C_Ruapehu%2C_New_Zealand_13.JPG. Michal Klajban [CC BY-SA 4.0 (https://creativecommons.org/licenses/by-sa/4.0)]

p.138 https://upload.wikimedia.org/wikipedia/commons/4/41/In_remembrance_of_the_Tangiwai_disaster%2C_60_years_ago_on_24_December_1953._%2811440413944%29.jpg. Archives New Zealand from New Zealand [CC BY-SA 2.0 (https://creativecommons.org/licenses/by-sa/2.0)]

p.139 https://www.wvencyclopedia.org/assets/0003/2682/Silver_Bridge.jpg. https://www.wvencyclopedia.org/assets/0003/3013/Silver_Bridge_wreckage.jpg, with permission' from West Virginia Humanities Council

Chapter 22

p.140 https://www.flickr.com/photos/sanbeiji/220646211. Bay Bridge by Joe Lewis Attribution-ShareAlike 2.0 Generic (CC BY-SA 2.0)

p.141 Sunshine Skyway Bridge with the ship that caused its collapse, 1980©AP Photo/Jackie Green

p.142 Big Bayou Canot Bridge with the barge that struck it, 1993, © AP Photo/Mark Foley, File

pp.142, 143 https://upload.wikimedia.org/wikipedia/commons/c/cc/Sunset_Limited_Big_Bayout_Canot.png National Transportation Safety Board [Public domain]

p.144 Clearing wreckage of the Eschede train disaster, 1998, © AP Photo/Jens Meyer

Chapter 23

p.145 https://upload.wikimedia.org/wikipedia/commons/7/79/San_Francisco%E2%80%93Oakland_Bay_Bridge-_New_and_Old_bridges.jpg© Frank Schulenburg / CC BY-SA 3.0

pp.146 147 https://upload.wikimedia.org/wikipedia/commons/c/c1/Telford_Clifton_Suspension_Bridge_plan.jpg Thomas Telford [Public domain]

Chapter 24

p.148 https://upload.wikimedia.org/wikipedia/commons/5/52/London_Millenium_Bridge_Tate_Modern_Museum_Saint_Paul%27s_Cathedral_Tamise_River_Night_Explore_Image_Picture_Long_pose_%2816484823825%29.jpg

mountain goat, https://upload.wikimedia.org/wikipedia/commons/thumb/1/16/Mountain_Goat_Mount_Massive.JPG/2048px-Mountain_Goat_Mount_Massive.JPG, Darklich14 [CC BY 3.0 (https://creativecommons.org/licenses/by/3.0)]

pika, https://en.wikipedia.org/wiki/File:American_pika_(ochotona_princeps)_with_a_mouthful_of_flowers.jpg#file Frédéric Dulude-de Broin (CC BY-SA 4.0)

squirrel, https://upload.wikimedia.org/wikipedia/commons/thumb/1/1c/Squirrel_posing.jpg/1225px-Squirrel_posing.jpg, Peter Trimming (CC BY 2.0)

pronghorn, https://upload.wikimedia.org/wikipedia/commons/thumb/f/f3/Pronghorn_Yellowstone_%28crop%29.jpg/2048px-Pronghorn_Yellowstone_%28crop%29.jpg, Thomas Wolf, www.foto-tw.de / Wikimedia Commons / CC BY-SA 3.0

toads, https://pixabay.com/photos/toad-frog-frog-pond-high-amphibian-3789845/ by PaulaPaulsen

salamander, https://upload.wikimedia.org/wikipedia/commons/thumb/1/15/Spotted_Salamander_2.jpg/2048px-Spotted_Salamander_2.jpg, Brian Gratwicke [CC BY 2.0 (https://creativecommons.org/licenses/by/2.0)]

trout, https://upload.wikimedia.org/wikipedia/commons/thumb/b/b9/Rainbow_Trout.jpg/1280px-Rainbow_Trout.jpg, The original uploader was JDG at English Wikipedia.Later version(s) were uploaded by Papa November at en.wikipedia.(Original text: NATIONAL CONSERVATION TRAINING CENTER-PUBLICATIONS AND TRAINING MATERIALS for US Fish and Wildlife Service) [Public domain]

lynx, https://upload.wikimedia.org/wikipedia/commons/0/0a/Canadian_lynx_by_Keith_Williams.jpg, kdee64 (Keith Williams) [CC BY 2.0 (https://creativecommons.org/licenses/by/2.0)]

mountain lion, https://upload.wikimedia.org/wikipedia/commons/4/45/Mountain_lion_Winter_%28cropped%29.jpg, CindyLouPhotos [CC BY 2.0 (https://creativecommons.org/licenses/by/2.0)]

wolf, https://www.flickr.com/photos/yellowstonenps/16239820971, Yellowstone National Park, public domain

wolverine, https://upload.wikimedia.org/wikipedia/commons/thumb/0/0d/Wolverine_01.jpg/1280px-Wolverine_01.jpg, William F. Wood [CC BY-SA 4.0 (https://creativecommons.org/licenses/by-sa/4.0)]

bobcat, https://upload.wikimedia.org/wikipedia/commons/d/dc/Bobcat2.jpg, Author:User:Calibas, public domain

South America

puma, https://upload.wikimedia.org/wikipedia/commons/thumb/4/4a/Puma_face.jpg/2048px-Puma_face.jpg, Bas Lammers [CC BY 2.0 (https://creativecommons.org/licenses/by/2.0)]

jaguar, https://upload.wikimedia.org/wikipedia/commons/thumb/4/4a/Puma_face.jpg/2048px-Puma_face.jpg, Bas Lammers [CC BY 2.0 (https://creativecommons.org/licenses/by/2.0)]

golden lion tamarin, https://upload.wikimedia.org/wikipedia/commons/8/87/Golden_lion_tamarin_portrait3.jpg, Jeroen Kransen [CC BY-SA 2.0 (https://creativecommons.org/licenses/by-sa/2.0)]

Europe

red deer, https://upload.wikimedia.org/wikipedia/commons/thumb/4/41/Red_deer_%28Cervus_elaphus%29_hind.jpg/1024px-Red_deer_%28Cervus_elaphus%29_hind.jpg, Charles J Sharp Attribution-ShareAlike 4.0 International (CC BY-SA 4.0)

roe deer, https://www.flickr.com/photos/76338186@N03/15249498842. Kumweni Attribution 2.0 Generic (CC BY 2.0)

hedgehog, https://upload.wikimedia.org/wikipedia/commons/thumb/7/72/Igel.JPG/1024px-Igel.JPG, Gibe [CC BY-SA 3.0 (http://creativecommons.org/licenses/by-sa/3.0/)]

wild boar, https://upload.wikimedia.org/wikipedia/commons/thumb/1/1d/Wild_Boar_Habbitat_2.jpg/1024px-Wild_Boar_Habbitat_2.jpg, Richard Bartz, Munich Makro Freak [CC BY-SA 2.5 (https://creativecommons.org/licenses/by-sa/2.5)]

red fox, https://upload.wikimedia.org/wikipedia/commons/thumb/e/ee/Red_Fox_%28Vulpes_vulpes%29_-British_Wildlife_Centre-8.jpg/2048px-Red_Fox_%28Vulpes_vulpes%29_-British_Wildlife_Centre-8.jpg, Keven Law [CC BY-SA 2.0 (https://creativecommons.org/licenses/by-sa/2.0)]

badger, https://pixabay.com/photos/badger-wildlife-english-nature-2030975/ by andyballard, Image by <a href="https://pixabay.com/users/andyballard-1141862/?utm_source=link-attribution&utm_medium=referral&utm_campaign=image&utm_content=2030975">andy ballard</a> from <a href="https://pixabay.com/?utm_source=link-attribution&utm_medium=referral&utm_campaign=image&utm_content=2030975">Pixabay</a>

water vole, https://upload.wikimedia.org/wikipedia/commons/thumb/9/9a/Water_Vole_%286038169781%29.jpg/1024px-Water_Vole_%286038169781%29.jpg, Peter Trimming from Croydon, England [CC BY 2.0 (https://creativecommons.org/licenses/by/2.0)]

marten, https://upload.wikimedia.org/wikipedia/commons/thumb/2/25/Martes_flavigula%2C_yellow-throated_marten.jpg/2048px-Martes_flavigula%2C_yellow-throated_marten.jpg, Rushenb [CC BY 2.0 (https://creativecommons.org/licenses/by/2.0)]

squirrel, https://upload.wikimedia.org/wikipedia/commons/4/4d/Central-european_squirrel.jpg, ufoncz [CC BY 2.0 (https://creativecommons.org/licenses/by/2.0)]

Asia

Lion-tailed macaque, https://upload.wikimedia.org/wikipedia/commons/thumb/f/f5/Lion-tailed_macaque_by_N_A_Nazeer.jpg/2048px-Lion-tailed_macaque_by_N_A_Nazeer.jpg, N. A. Naseer / www.nilgirimarten.com / naseerart@gmail.com [CC BY-SA 2.5 in (https://creativecommons.org/licenses/by-sa/2.5/in/deed.en)]

Africa

https://pxhere.com/en/photo/615275, public domain

Australia

wallaby, https://www.flickr.com/photos/dj-dwayne/4426946928, by Dwayne Madden Attribution 2.0 Generic (CC BY 2.0)

kangaroo, https://upload.wikimedia.org/wikipedia/commons/thumb/0/03/Kangaroo_Australia_01_11_2008_-_retouch2.jpg/2048px-Kangaroo_Australia_01_11_2008_-_retouch2.jpg, Patrol110, based on image by User:Lilly M [CC BY-SA 3.0 (http://creativecommons.org/licenses/by-sa/3.0/)]

bandicoot, Long-nosed bandicoot https://upload.wikimedia.org/wikipedia/commons/thumb/a/a2/Long-nosed_Bandicoot_JCB.jpg/2048px-Long-nosed_Bandicoot_JCB.jpg, Joseph C Boone [CC BY-SA 4.0 (https://creativecommons.org/licenses/by-sa/4.0)]

possum, https://upload.wikimedia.org/wikipedia/commons/2/22/Trichosurus_vulpecula_1.jpg
JJ Harrison (https://www.jjharrison.com.au/), (Creative Commons CC-BY-SA-2.5)

wombat, https://upload.wikimedia.org/wikipedia/commons/1/18/Vombatus_ursinus_-Maria_Island_National_Park.jpg, JJ Harrison (jjharrison89@facebook.com). Attribution-ShareAlike 3.0 Unported (CC BY-SA 3.0)

red crab, https://upload.wikimedia.org/wikipedia/commons/thumb/5/56/Christmas_Island_%285774532171%29.jpg/2048px-Christmas_Island_%285774532171%29.jpg, DIAC images [CC BY 2.0 (https://creativecommons.org/licenses/by/2.0)]

bats, https://upload.wikimedia.org/wikipedia/commons/thumb/9/9b/6A5A6458.jpg/2048px-6A5A6458.jpg, Andreas Trepte [CC BY-SA 4.0 (https://creativecommons.org/licenses/by-sa/4.0)]

reptiles, https://upload.wikimedia.org/wikipedia/commons/thumb/9/93/Perentie_Lizard_Perth_Zoo_SMC_Spet_2005.jpg/2048px-Perentie_Lizard_Perth_Zoo_SMC_Spet_2005.jpg, SeanMack [CC BY-SA 3.0 (http://creativecommons.org/licenses/by-sa/3.0/)]

Chapter 26

p.164 https://upload.wikimedia.org/wikipedia/commons/7/77/Kiev_-_bridge_construction.jpg. Tiia Monto [CC BY-SA 3.0 (https://creativecommons.org/licenses/by-sa/3.0)]

p.166 https://upload.wikimedia.org/wikipedia/commons/a/a0/Pabell%C3%B3n-Puente_Zaragoza.jpg Grez [CC BY-SA 3.0 (https://creativecommons.org/licenses/by-sa/3.0)]

p.168 top https://www.geograph.org.uk/more.php?id=3186941© Copyright frank smith, Attribution-ShareAlike 2.0 Generic (CC BY-SA 2.0)

p.168 bottom. FRP bridge, https://www.fibercore-europe.com/en/products/bicycle-bridges/, with permission of FiberCore Europe.

Chapter 27

p.169 MX3D Printed Bridge 2018 Photo by Thijs Wolzak 2, with permission of MX3D.

p.170 https://www.flickr.com/photos/80651083@N00/2830284651. Apple Valley Road Bridge, Lyons, Colorado, Thaddeus Roan. Attribution 2.0 Generic (CC BY 2.0)

p.171 background https://upload.wikimedia.org/wikipedia/commons/thumb/5/54/Bamboo_grove_-_Eish%C5%8D-ji_-_Kamakura%2C_Kanagawa%2C_Japan_-_DSC08150.JPG/4096px-Bamboo_grove_-_Eish%C5%8D-ji_-_Kamakura%2C_Kanagawa%2C_Japan_-_DSC08150.JPG. Daderot [CC0]

Index

AI generated picture of Mao Yisheng's Statue at CMU, by Barnas Monteith and Mao Yahan 茅亚涵

Acknowledgments

Special thanks to the Mao Yisheng Foundation for inspiring and supporting this project. I also want to express my appreciation to Sarah Christian, Assistant Teaching Professor of Civil and Environmental Engineering at Carnegie Mellon University, for her technical advice and review of this book. Sarah clarified my understanding and steered me clear of errors; those that remain are all my own. I also wish to thank Eugene H. Pool for his careful reading and helpful comments.

Finally, this book would not have been possible without the steady support and creative design of my Tumblehome partners, Barnas Monteith and Yu-Yi Ling.

About the Author

Pendred Noyce has written or co-written fourteen books for young people, both fiction and nonfiction, mostly about science. She practiced as a doctor of internal medicine, helped lead a national foundation for math and science education, and happily raised five children. She lives in Boston and Maine.

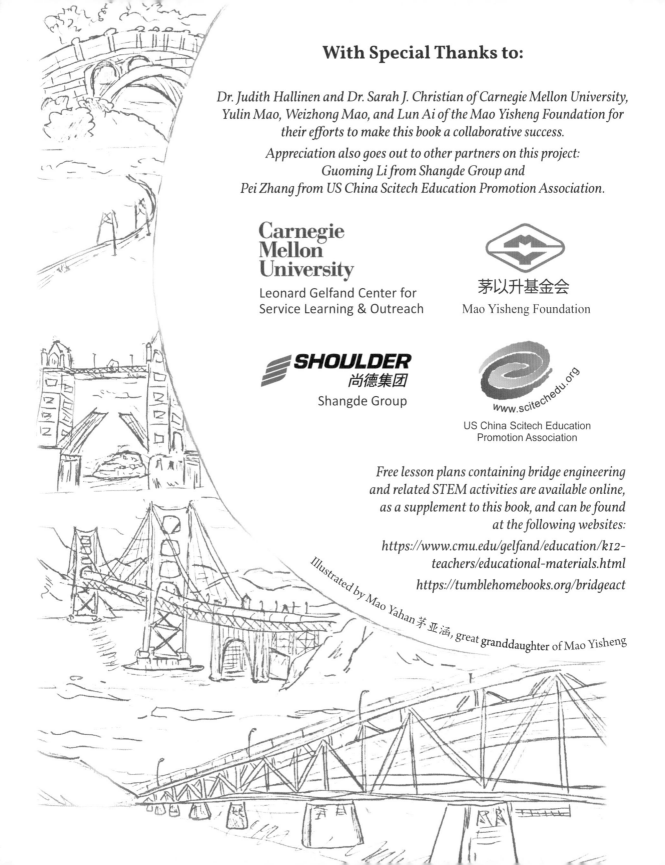

With Special Thanks to:

*Dr. Judith Hallinen and Dr. Sarah J. Christian of Carnegie Mellon University,
Yulin Mao, Weizhong Mao, and Lun Ai of the Mao Yisheng Foundation for
their efforts to make this book a collaborative success.*

*Appreciation also goes out to other partners on this project:
Guoming Li from Shangde Group and
Pei Zhang from US China Scitech Education Promotion Association.*

**Carnegie
Mellon
University**
Leonard Gelfand Center for
Service Learning & Outreach

茅以升基金会
Mao Yisheng Foundation

SHOULDER
尚德集团
Shangde Group

www.scitechedu.org
US China Scitech Education
Promotion Association

*Free lesson plans containing bridge engineering
and related STEM activities are available online,
as a supplement to this book, and can be found
at the following websites:*

*https://www.cmu.edu/gelfand/education/k12-
teachers/educational-materials.html*

https://tumblehomebooks.org/bridgeact

Illustrated by Mao Yahan 茅亚涵, great granddaughter of Mao Yisheng

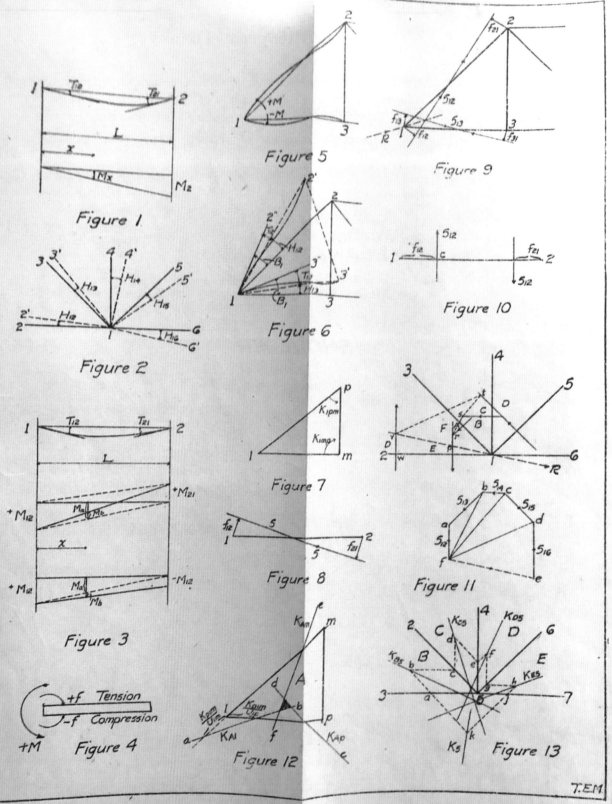

Figure 1

Figure 2

Figure 3

Figure 4

Figure 5

Figure 6

Figure 7

Figure 8

Figure 9

Figure 10

Figure 11

Figure 12

Figure 13

+f Tension
−f Compression

Bridge blueprints sketches drawn by Mao Yisheng, provided by the Mao Yisheng Foundation.

PLATE 1